No More
Cold
Calling™

NO MORE COLD CALLING™

The Breakthrough System That Will Leave Your Competition in the Dust

JOANNE S. BLACK

WARNER
BUSINESS
BOOKS™

NEW YORK   BOSTON

Warner Business Books
Warner Books

Time Warner Book Group
1271 Avenue of the Americas, New York, NY 10020
Visit our Web site at www.twbookmark.com.

The Warner Business Books logo is a trademark of Warner Books.

Printed in the United States of America

First Edition: April 2006

10   9   8   7   6   5   4   3   2   1

Library of Congress Cataloging-in-Publication Data
Black, Joanne S.
    No more cold calling : the breakthrough system that will leave your
competition in the dust/ Joanne S. Black.
        p. cm.
    ISBN-13: 978-0-446-57779-3
    ISBN-10: 0-446-57779-0
    1. Selling. 2. Business referrals. I. Title.
    HF5438.25.B545 2006
    658.85—dc22   2005022565

Book design by Charles Sutherland

I dedicate this book to my Aunt Gert.
There will never be anyone like her in this world.

Gertrude Schlesinger Leibowitz
November 29, 1910–August 2, 2004

In Memoriam—My Parents

Eunice Green Schlesinger
Nathan Samuel Schlesinger

Who never lived to share the joys of my life.

ACKNOWLEDGMENTS

None of us would be where we are or who we are without our family and dear friends.

My husband, Bruce—who loves me no matter what I look like or what I do—who tells me every day how proud he is of me.

My daughter Judy—who lights up every room she enters. She is my friend, my inspiration, and my final editor.

My daughter Dana—who has been my Business Buddy for the last six years; who I can call anytime for advice, and who is one of the greatest actors who ever lived.

My grandson, Max—who has brought me joy beyond my wildest dreams.

My sons-in-law, Adam and Brent—two of the best guys in the world who celebrate my accomplishments as if I were their own mother.

My sister, Jill—who asks me every week, "When are we going on the book tour?" She is my dearest friend and travel buddy.

My Aunt Leona and Uncle Joel—who are my second parents, and who have always delighted in my family and my achievements. They are truly young at heart.

My Aunt Ruthie and Uncle David, Aunt Marilyn and Uncle Milton—whose love for each other and our family has been an inspiration to me.

My dear friends, Susan and Jane—whose friendship and encouragement are unparalleled. They are my own private cheerleading section.

My friends in Women in Business, San Francisco Chamber Business Alliance, and National Association of Women Business Owners—who kept asking me, "How's the book coming?"

My mentor, Gerry Sindell at Thought Leaders Intl.—who stretched my thinking beyond belief and coached me to write the best book I could.

My agent, Matthew Carnicelli of Carnicelli Literary Management—who saw the possibilities for this book immediately, and who found the perfect publisher.

My editor, Rick Wolff at Warner Books—who gave me exactly the feedback I needed, who kept me on track, and who always understood that "life happens."

CONTENTS

No More
Cold
Calling™

Get Ready for a Great Adventure!

I've been hearing wonderful things about you." Don't you love hearing that? Now picture a sales world where you will only be meeting clients who want to meet with you—a world in which you'll never have to cold call again, send prospecting letters, or entice clients with special offers. Enter the world of referral selling.

In this new world you'll spend your time wisely, you'll be working less and getting more, and you'll have fabulous clients, more revenue, and more profits. You'll be transforming the way you work and experiencing a different way of life as a professional salesperson. Once you experience the kind of success referral selling brings, there's no turning back.

If you have all the clients you want and they are all profitable clients, then you don't need to read this book. If 100 percent of your business is referral business and you have more clients than you can handle, you don't need to read this book. But if you don't fit into either of these categories, then be ready to read this book and to do some hard but deeply satisfying work.

The Focus

There are really just two parts to sales: Part one is getting in front of the right people, and part two is everything that happens after that.

The focus of most sales efforts is on part two—conducting a sales call, asking probing questions, proposing, presenting, and closing. How much time and energy do you typically spend thinking about part one—getting in front of the right people? Probably very little. Think about it. If you don't get in front of the right people nothing else really matters, does it? You might be thinking of that dreaded term prospecting, when you think about getting in front of the right people—and you envision yourself cold calling on the phone, following up on dead leads, or calling door-to-door. It doesn't have to be like that.

What You'll Need

Referral selling is logical and simple, but it's not easy. Otherwise, everyone would be doing it. You'll need to start using several new skills as you make the transition to referral selling. The rewards, fortunately, are almost instantaneous: better customers, better sales, and a less stressful work life.

DEDICATION

You will need the courage and guts to transform the way you sell, and you will need to dedicate time to learn, practice, and implement a Referral-Selling System. It is a rigorous discipline that will give you a monumental return on your investment.

THE PERSONAL TOUCH

You'll need to get connected and stay connected. We're all linked to technology more than ever before. Many of us spend more time talking on our cell phones, checking e-mail, or showing off the bells and whistles of our latest gadgets than we do actually connecting with people, especially new people.

Selling is personal—very, very personal. We need to be present, involved, and connected. We need to connect—one human being to the other. It's then that we can make the person-to-person sale. Technology is a support for our sales process, not a substitute.

AN OPEN MIND

You're about to begin an exciting adventure. My passion is to transform the way you work. Change isn't easy. You need to be open to throwing traditional sales models out the door, to challenging practices that aren't working, and to enrolling others in the Referral-Selling System.

One of my first lessons about working differently in the business world was at Joseph Magnin—a women's specialty store in San Francisco. It was my first job out of college, and I entered their management training program. I wanted to re-arrange a display of elegant gifts, and I asked some of the older employees what they thought of the idea. They all told me that it had never been done before. I went to my manager and told her what I wanted to do. When I mentioned the fact that everyone told me it had never been done before, she looked at me and said, "That's the best reason I know for doing it." I was twenty-two years old, and I have never forgotten what my manager told me. She probably had no clue what an impression she made on me.

Since that time I continue to challenge traditional ways of working. I challenge tired prospecting techniques like cold calling, direct mail campaigns, advertising, and trade shows—and the expectation that these activities will bring us great clients.

There's an old story about a young girl who watched her mother cut off the ends of a ham before she put it in the roasting pan. One day the little girl asked her mother why she cut off the ends of the ham. The mother thought for a moment and said, "I don't know. My mother always did it that way. Why don't you ask your grandmother?" So the little girl asked her grandmother why she cut off the ends of the ham before she put it in the pan. The grandmother said, "That's simple. The pan wasn't big enough."

I invite you to ask yourself why you are selling the way you are selling. If what you are doing is giving you the life you want, keep doing it. Otherwise, have an open mind, enjoy your reading, and catch the Referral Spirit!

CHAPTER 1

Catch the Referral Spirit

Selling is the best job in the world.

We can solve problems for our clients, be instrumental in helping them grow their businesses, engage in robust discussions, expand their thinking, and build amazing relationships. No other job gives us the opportunity to truly connect with others and to plug into the pulse of the economy from anywhere in the world.

Referral selling is the best way to create these vibrant relationships. "Hold the phone!" you might say. "There are lots of things I do that can bring me new customers." Really? Like attending trade shows, sending direct mail, and cold calling? Most sales professionals will tell you that trade-show leads are next to useless, and direct mail has an average 3 percent return. Cold calling has a 2 percent return for your time. In addition, you usually don't reach the right people, and your sales cycle drags on for so long that in far too many instances, your contacts will have moved to new jobs before you ever see an order.

Compare that to a typical occasion when you received a qualified referral. What percent of the time did you close the deal? If you're like most people, it was 80 or 90 percent. No one, and I mean no one, has ever told me it's less than 50 percent. And take a moment to think about how you felt when you contacted the person who'd been referred to you. You immediately entered into a robust business conversation, you knocked the competition out of contention without the objections you typically receive, and you closed the deal quickly without price resistance. You experienced a taste of the Referral Spirit.

Referral Spirit is the excitement you feel when you're working with the right customers. You become supercharged when you're face-to-face or having a vigorous conversation on the phone. You are present, energized, and know you're doing great work. I want you to have this feeling all the time, and I'm going to show you how.

The Referral Spirit is the glorious part of the world of selling, where having fewer prospects is better, because those new prospects are *qualified*. That's the power of referral selling.

Referral Selling Is HOT!

In referral selling you are introduced to people you want to meet and who want to meet you. You create the business opportunity that is yours to win. You are meeting with people who may become your customers or who may be your advocates within their organization. Either way, you are starting with someone on your side.

- *Success Rate:* Your success rate will skyrocket because you will be converting prospects to clients between 50 and 90 percent of the time.
- *Building Customer Relationships:* You will do more business with existing customers, and they will become loyal referral sources for you.
- *Your Customer Is Pre-sold,* so you'll shorten the sales cycle: You will close your sales faster, because your customers will already know who you are and will want to work with you.
- *Reducing the Competition:* The competition either diminishes or becomes nonexistent, because you are the one who will now set the standard against which others must compete. Because you have an established relationship, your client will quickly share important information with you.

Creating Trust

When a customer comes to you through a referral, you are credible the minute you answer the phone or when the customer walks through your door. You have the kind of robust conversation that you love—learning about the client's business and ways you can solve his problems. When you've been referred, you know that the customer is qualified because you've already specified your Ideal Customer. (More about this later.)

Wouldn't it be great if *all* of your business came from referrals? Wouldn't you rather *take* a sales call than *make* a sales call? You'll save time, work with people you like, close deals faster, and, above all, you'll enjoy yourself. That kind of selling is fun. It's about caring for customers and always proposing the best solution for them.

Successful Salespeople Don't Just Happen

Whether you are cold calling most of the time now and getting lucky with the occasional referral or your business is already mostly from referrals, you are going to be a different kind of salesperson after you read this book. Unless your business right now is 100 percent from referrals, you are spending too much time on sales activities that aren't giving you the payoff you deserve.

I learned an important lesson recently. A participant who attended one of my No More Cold Calling™ workshops was the president of a successful company. He had been in business for twenty years, and 98 percent of his business came from referrals. Everyone asked him, "Why are you here?" His answer: "I want to get better, and I want to purposefully attract the kind of clients where we can deliver our best work." I was reminded again that successful people continue to invest in themselves and their companies. They understand that they can and must always get better.

So, if what you're doing is working for you, by all means keep doing it. If not, then invest your time in learning a new way of working that will send your sales skyrocketing.

I have been selling and managing sales teams for over

thirty-five years, and I have developed definite points of view on many subjects related to sales. My clients tell me that they pay me for my opinions and points of view. I will share many of these insights with you in this book. Feel free to disagree. But in your effort to work smarter, I encourage you to have an open mind.

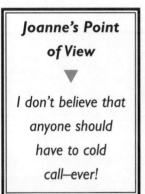

Joanne's Point of View

▼

I don't believe that anyone should have to cold call—ever!

The Cold Reality of Cold Calling

I define cold calling as contacting someone who does not know you and who is not expecting your call. Cold calls can be made on the phone, in person, by fax, by direct mail, or by e-mail.

How many salespeople really like to make cold calls and are good at it? In my informal research over the last seven years in business groups and in my workshops, when I ask this question to groups that range from twenty to two hundred participants, usually only one or two people raise their hands. Generally, other sales experts have informally confirmed that only about 2 percent of all salespeople enjoy making cold calls. And the funny thing is, even some of them are still attending my No More Cold Calling presentations. So maybe even these cold-calling veterans don't really love it all that much.

So at least 98 percent of salespeople dislike making cold calls. Yet many salespeople are still cold calling. Why? I hear many responses: "It's habit," "I don't know any other way," "I actually get clients," or "My boss makes me do it."

Here are some comments *Fast Company* collected from

salespeople about cold calling. What is your opinion when you read these statements? (My comments follow each one.)

- *"I don't mind getting myself 'bloodied' cold calling."*

Really? Why would you want to do this to yourself?

- *"Cold calling is the sales professional's mantra."*

Who told you this was the way you had to work?

- *"Cold calling will never die. It may change, but not die."*

It *has* died with business-to-consumer marketing. The public is averse to cold callers, and their displeasure will continue to increase.

- *"Cold calling is absolutely a critical selling tool. It allows growing companies the chance in a lifetime to land a big customer early in the game."*

In fact, cold calling is the *least* effective way of landing a big customer.

- *"Cold calling is a good way to fill the pipeline with good quality leads."*

Quality? Cold-called leads are the least qualified, and they're the ones most likely to die in the pipeline.

- *"Cold calling is a necessary evil. It gets your name out there so at least a potential customer has some familiarity with your company and what you offer."*

Why do you do things that are "a necessary evil"? Just getting people familiar with your company and what you offer is not making a sale.

- *"The secret to cold calling is that you have to have a solution for customers."*

It's not a secret. *Every* sale requires that we have a solution. What would we be selling if we didn't have a solution? Underwater basket-weaving lessons?

- *"The more calls you make, the easier it becomes."*

The same could be said for banging your head against a wall. If you keep doing it, will it hurt less? Will it become easier to do? Maybe, but it's still a waste of time.

Why We Cold Call

Salespeople tell me that they have many reasons for cold calling.

It's habit. Isn't it amazing how you continue to do things that you know don't yield the results you want? Benjamin

Franklin defined insanity as "doing the same thing over and over and expecting different results."

I don't know any other way. Actually, you do. It's that really nice thing that happens once in a while when out of the blue a new customer calls because someone referred him to you.

I actually get clients. Sure you do. But if you could get five times as many clients by doing a fraction of the work, would you continue to cold call?

My boss makes me do it. Think of your boss and other seasoned salespeople. Are they cold calling? No. Then why are they asking you to do it? Too many sales managers have made cold calling a "rite of passage." They suffered through it, so now you have to as well.

My boss can measure my activity. There are metrics for cold calling, so it's easy to manage. How many times have you heard, "It's a numbers game." Let's examine what those numbers are. People who cold call tell me that if they make one hundred calls, they will actually speak with twenty to twenty-five people, set ten to twelve appointments, and if they're lucky, close one to two deals.

The "Warm Call" Fantasy

Salespeople tell me all the time that they're not really making cold calls—they're making "warm calls." I don't agree. A sales call is either cold or hot. We're deluding ourselves into thinking we're not cold calling, so we say that we're making warm calls.

Consider the following situations:

- You call someone because you got the name from a colleague or friend. Cold!
- You call someone and then follow up with a letter. Cold!
- The person's name came from a specific list. Still cold!

These are all cold calls—the person doesn't know you and is not expecting your call. Even though you think you've been able to avoid sounding like a telemarketer, it's still a cold call.

In 2003 Huthwaite (www.huthwaite.com) surveyed buyers about their attitudes on prospecting: Ninety-one percent of buyers never respond to an unsolicited inquiry, 88 percent will have nothing to do with cold callers, and 94 percent couldn't remember a single prospector or message they had received during the previous two years. Obviously cold calls aren't working. With such dismal results, why would you ever cold call? Why would you even settle for the illusion of a warm call? A call is *hot* when you have an introduction. Nothing else counts. Nothing else matters.

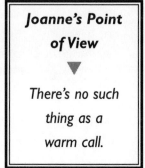

Joanne's Point of View

▼

There's no such thing as a warm call.

Moving On

As you use this book, you will begin to shift your relationship with referrals from what many people call "word of mouth" (something that's always great when it happens: "I just got a call from a new customer who was referred to me") to something you *make* happen. It won't matter whether you are just starting out or if you are already a veteran salesperson or sales manager, part of a large organization or a sole proprietor; in a business with a short or a long sales cycle; in high tech or in consulting; a Realtor who depends on timing or an office-supply salesperson dealing with people who always need what you sell; selling business-to-business or business-to-consumer; or selling face-to-face or on the phone. No More Cold Calling is universal.

Catching the Referral Spirit means that you will consciously and enthusiastically be giving referrals as well as receiving them—referring without expecting that someone will give you something in return. You are generous and truly want to help others. Doesn't it feel great to put good people together? You bet it does.

The Referral Queen

I am the Referral Queen. I have a banner to prove it, and I travel with my crown and scepter. I have built my business solely on referrals. And yet even when people know what I do, they still ask me how I get my clients. Most people find it unbelievable that I have built a successful business totally on referrals. The fact is, I won't do business with anyone unless I've been referred—whether it's for business or for personal services.

Because I am always giving referrals, people ask me all the time for referrals to other business services. Finally, I decided to list them on my website under the "Partner" tab. Here is a

message that I got from Paula Doubleday (www.pdoubleday
.com), a graphic artist who helped me when my business was
young:

> I've got a funny story for you. I got a call yesterday
> from a woman who used to work for a major clothing
> manufacturer. I did some work for her in 1994. She left to
> start her own consulting company, and I did her logo and
> collateral. Then she moved back to New Jersey in '95. She
> called yesterday out of the blue. She has three companies
> now, and they have been working with an ad agency on
> some new logos but it just wasn't working. So somebody
> asks her who did the original logo. And, hey, let's call her.
> So she "Googles" me, and what comes up first but *your
> site,* Joanne! And on it you've been kind enough to put my
> phone number. So the woman calls me! Thanks for hav-
> ing my name there!

Now it's time for you to catch the Referral Spirit and make a
referral of your own. Think of people you could help by referring them to one of your favorite service providers. It could be
personal referrals to your mechanic, massage therapist, or hair-
dresser. You could make business referrals to an IT consultant,
customer relationship management (CRM) solution provider,
accounting firm, web designer, sales consultant, or computer
software program that's saved you tons of time.

Share your referrals with others, and they'll start sharing
theirs with you. Connect with people you haven't spoken to in
a while. Find out what they're doing. You'll end up with the

most excellent resources, and you'll be richer for the interaction.

Note: To make a change in your life and in the way your company does business, you will need to take action. Otherwise it's all just talk. So throughout this book you'll find Action Steps. You don't have to take them all (some might not even apply to you or your organization). But if you don't take at least 80 percent of them, there's not much of a chance you can transition to referral selling.

Here's your first Action Step:

ACTION STEP 1

Make a Referral
Contact one or two people you know, find out what they need, and make a referral.

You will begin to see that referral selling is the only way to build the kind of relationships that create loyal customers who are then thrilled to refer others to you. Think of it as having your own private sales force out there working just for you.

What a concept!

CHAPTER 2

Buckle Up!

You can become a referral-selling powerhouse. To do it you'll need to buckle up and accelerate your thinking. You'll be moving quickly down a new and exciting road. Four elements are essential to making the transition to referral selling. But neglect any one of them, and you'll swiftly fall back into the dark pit of cold calling (not that I'm trying to scare you or anything).

The four essentials:

Attitude
Strategy
Accountability
Process

> **ASAP**

ATTITUDE

I asked you in the first chapter to try and keep an open mind. Now, are you ready to commit to certain activities that will take you from where you are now to where you want to go? You need to be firm in your willingness to completely and fairly test whether referral selling will become your silver bullet. You must be unwavering in your commitment, because you will come across those who will try to talk you out of it. They will tell you that referral selling takes too long, that you still need to cold call, or that it seems too touchy-feely. Rubbish.

STRATEGY

In 1996 when I founded my current company, I surveyed salespeople, sales managers, and business owners regarding their sales strategies. Everyone had a marketing strategy, a financial strategy, and a product strategy. The sales strategy—if there was one—was buried in a cumbersome business plan. When I asked this same group about referrals, they all told me that they, too, loved referrals. But when I asked if they had an intentional strategy to build their business through referrals, I discovered that almost no one had figured out a way to build a 100-percent referral-based business. That was when I knew No More Cold Calling was going to fill a huge need.

My first challenge was to understand why, if referrals are so great, most companies aren't doing something on a regular basis to increase them. I discovered that there are four reasons that prevent companies from using their most powerful potential sales strategy.

1. It's a new skill. There aren't a lot of salespeople who know how to ask for referrals in a way that gets them

immediately in front of the people they want to meet and who want to meet them.

2. People are uncomfortable with the idea of asking others for referrals. They feel that they may jeopardize a relationship, that it feels pushy, or that the other person might say no.
3. They aren't aware that there are metrics for referrals, as there are for cold calling, direct mail, and advertising.
4. They don't have a disciplined process or methodology to support referral selling—from incorporating referrals into their sales process to rewarding and compensating people for referral activities.

The key to referral selling is that it requires us to ask existing clients, friends, and other contacts to make a referral. Asking for a referral is a very personal event. We often feel that we're making ourselves vulnerable when we ask, because someone might refuse the request. That's a different kind of rejection than we're used to getting when cold calling! This is more personal.

Some people think they've already tried referral selling but haven't been successful. Without knowing how to ask for referrals, the chances of succeeding in building a system that will continue to work are not very good. You and your sales team will need to learn the skills of knowing how to ask.

You can begin to see that adopting a Referral-Selling System has some genuine challenges. A wise client told me that transitioning to referral selling is simple, but it isn't easy.

Accountability

Look back at your own training history. How many times have you been to a training session, left all hyped up and eager to get started, but a week later realized that you'd abandoned or forgotten most of what you were so excited about? Or perhaps you tried to apply what you learned but were given other assignments or were told to continue what you used to do. Often, you didn't take the time to apply your new learning, and no one followed up with you. Before long, you gave up on the new approach. It was just easier to do things the old way. We've all been there.

We need sales managers who support and coach us. When we adopt the Referral-Selling System, the way success is measured changes, because there are metrics for referral-selling activities as well as for referral-selling results. If you and your managers agree on the key activities that will get sales results, then you need to celebrate when you've been successful at those activities.

Managers have a pivotal role in making the referral process work. But in addition, we need to be accountable not only to our managers but to ourselves, and to someone outside of our organization who we know and respect. You will need to identify your Business Buddy—your personal reinforcement system.

You need to recognize that you can't master referral selling by yourself. Look at successful salespeople you know—it doesn't matter in what industry: high-tech, financial services, consulting, transportation, energy, or accounting. What do they all have in common? They use every available resource to help them sustain their success. In times when resources are scarce, the high achievers have no problem getting people to work on their teams. In fact, they usually have people lined up behind them.

You will need help and support to get to the point where you'll blow your old numbers away. You will need a Business Buddy: an individual, preferably a peer, whom you can talk to as often as necessary while you're getting started.

Choose someone who is a selling professional, just as you are, and who has a hunger to improve her skills and aggressively build her business.

Make sure it's someone you respect and who respects you. It is best if this person is not in the same business you are. You can trade war stories, and your differences will give each of you a fresh perspective. It doesn't matter where your Business Buddy is geographically, because modern technology eliminates distance. Whether you are a CEO, a vice president of sales, a salesperson, or a business owner; whether new to business or a veteran, a Business Buddy will keep you on track through the process.

Have someone in mind? Good. I want you to call right away and tell this person that you've decided to stop ineffective prospecting techniques and to become a referral-selling expert. You expect to raise your monthly sales by at least 30 percent, and you think this person would benefit by shifting to referral selling. If the person agrees to be your Business Buddy (and, of course, you will be hers), encourage the person to adopt a referral-selling strategy as well.

ACTION STEP 2

Find Your Business Buddy

Your meetings can be in-person or on the phone. Plan to spend thirty to fifty minutes each week, and set a specific date and time. Each of you will discuss your objectives for the meeting. Decide on ground rules—confidentiality of information and how feedback should be given and received. Tell the other person your business challenges, provide feedback, brainstorm strategic options, and agree and commit to action steps for the coming week.

PROCESS

I am the first person who runs screaming from a room when people start talking about the need for "process." It drives me nuts. As a salesperson all I want to do is to be with my clients. Please don't make me memorize a process that doesn't fit with my clients. Don't make me fill out a lot of paperwork. Just let me do my job. That being said, I have great respect for a strategic process. I'm willing to agree that there are certain essential steps, and if I stick to them, they will greatly enhance my chances for continued success.

It would be great if you could simply read this book, listen to one of my tapes, or attend my workshop and suddenly be transformed into a referral-selling expert. The fact is that's not likely to happen. My experience in helping hundreds of people shift to referral selling is that everyone does better if they consistently follow a straightforward methodology. You do need a process.

The challenge you face will not be learning my Referral-

Selling System. The difficulty will be in making the transition. You will build your skills, establish new metrics, get over any discomfort you have about asking for referrals, and begin to integrate referral selling into the way you work. When you get through the transition process, you'll never need to cold call again, your sales will take off, and you'll love what you're doing more than ever.

So how can you be certain about getting from here to there? Here are the essential components of the Referral-Selling System:

The Breakthrough Referral-Selling System

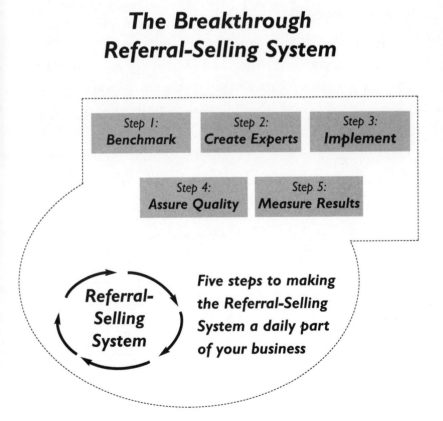

1. Benchmark

You've heard the term: Slow down to go fast. Before you go out there and blaze new trails, you need to decide on the trail you want to follow. What are your orga-

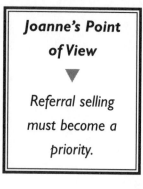

Joanne's Point of View

▼

Referral selling must become a priority.

nization's sales climate, sales process, metrics for success, and referral-selling goals? I always ask my clients what percent of their current business comes from referrals. Surprisingly, few can answer that question. Most say, "I don't know, but I should." The time you spend quickly assessing where you are now will help you avoid mistakes in the long run.

You will also need to get the buy-in of key people in your company. They must understand that agreeing to adopt a referral process is vastly different from implementing a referral process. The challenge is always in the execution. How many times have you seen companies adopt a new strategy, but nothing changes? It's just the flavor of the month, and no one pays much attention. Success in referral selling means setting priorities and driving accountability. Are you and your executives passionate about being the champions of the process? If the answer is yes, go to the next step.

If you're unsure, it's best to stop now. If you have the passion but your executive team does not, perhaps you need to find another job. If you're the executive and the rest of your team is not passionate, then you need to take a look at your leadership capabilities. How well are you positioning the "what's in it for them"?

ACTION STEP 3

Referral Assessment

- Do a quick assessment of referral sales in your organization.
- Discuss referral selling with your sales executives.

Determine what percent of your business currently comes from referrals. Do you have metrics for referrals? Are people rewarded for generating referrals? Are your group members willing to make a shift? Will they participate in the process and hold themselves as well as you accountable for getting referrals?

Everyone in your organization must be jazzed about referrals. They need to know that the company is becoming a referral-selling organization. Schedule a kick-off meeting. Outline the referral process. Let people know what's involved and that the way their efforts will be measured and rewarded will shift. Be clear about your expectations and communicate that the entire organization, including senior management, will be accountable for asking for and making referrals.

2. Create Experts

Ensure that you and your team know how to ask for referrals. Build skills in referral selling, develop sales messages that help you stand apart from competitors, create a profile of your Ideal Customer, and build a plan to attract and retain your best and most profitable customers.

3. Implement

Clarify roles and responsibilities, align reinforcement systems, build management competencies to manage the transition to referral selling, and create individual referral-selling plans. Implementing a plan is always the toughest part of any new process. Pay attention to the details, and monitor the transition climate.

4. Assure Quality

The only way you will achieve immediate results is with consistent reinforcement of the referral skills and the process. Create accountability, recognize and reward success, and continue to coach salespeople on referral behaviors. Work with your management team to keep the referral spirit going, and guarantee that referral selling becomes hardwired into your organization.

5. Measure Results

The return on your investment can now be measured by increases in revenue, profitability, and new clients—as well as decreases in your cost of sales. Make sure that you can track referrals in your database. Post and celebrate referral activities and results.

Now your organization is changing the way it conducts business. Managers and executives are developing metrics, reinforcing skills, and executing sales strategies that support their brand-new referral-selling organization. Referral activities are becoming integrated into the sales process, and everyone in the company has a role in generating referrals.

Your customers, your peers, and your alliance partners will all be your de facto sales team. The No More Cold Calling Referral-Selling System will start working for you. You will change the way you approach sales and the way you measure success. You will have a plan, goals, and simple metrics. Above all you will have a new enthusiasm, because from now on you will be talking to people you want to meet and who want to meet you. You will close sales faster and will have exactly the kind of clients who will be profitable for your company.

You and your organization will transition to a Referral-Selling System—a disciplined and powerful methodology to quickly obtain new clients as well as expand the business you have with existing clients.

Attitude, Strategy, Accountability, Process: **ASAP.** That's how quickly you can be on your way to becoming a referral-selling expert!

CHAPTER 3

Round Up the Usual Suspects (and Get Rid of Them)

I spoke with a client recently, I'll call him Ben, who told me that he had four categories of people in his database: suspects, prospects, clients, and dead. Ben is highly organized and proud of his ability to segment his follow-up calls. I asked him the difference between suspects and prospects. Suspects were names from one of the lists his company had purchased. He was frustrated with this list, because he would call and call but still couldn't reach people after six to ten calls. It was becoming harder and harder for Ben to pick up the phone to go after suspects.

Prospects were completely different. Prospects were people who had been referred to Ben, and when he called them, Ben was able to get an appointment immediately. I asked Ben why he was spending so much time trying to connect with suspects when he didn't even know if they had a need for his product. Silence. "What if you only had prospects to contact?" I asked. "What difference would *that* make in your business?"

It hadn't occurred to Ben that it was possible not to have suspects at all. What about you? If you understand the value of referral selling and the staggering waste that goes with cold calling, you'll want to put your energy into referral selling. That's not just a mental change or an attitude change. It means you will need to change the things you do every day and how you spend your time. It means that you must have total trust in the referral-selling process and in the referral activities that will ensure you attract more clients. At first this might seem unrealistic or even overwhelming. Imagine: You won't have to do all the painful stuff anymore. You may even find yourself working less and enjoying it way more.

Most people are fearful of changing the way they work or of relying solely on one method of prospecting. They feel as if the rug is being pulled out from under them. They won't have their reliable, proven statistics any more. Their boss may also be telling them to cold call—either by phone or on foot. (If your boss won't let you quit cold calling, you can still begin your own transformation by shifting to referral selling in your discretionary time. Ask for at least one referral a day, and your sales life will begin to change.)

Let's think about Ben for a moment. Three things would happen to Ben if he stopped spending time cold calling his suspects: He would get more business faster and thus earn more money. He would have the prestige of being the top salesperson in the company for the third year in a row. And he would have a renewed enthusiasm for his work.

"A renewed enthusiasm?" you say. "I thought all salespeople loved to sell." We do, but what we love the most is having significant business discussions with our customers. We don't like dialing for dollars, leaving a multitude of voicemails, and getting zero response. With cold-calling activities slowly grinding us down, how could we *not* eventually lose our gusto? We get discouraged, we begin to sound discouraged, and inevitably our entire sales performance takes a nosedive. We may even consider leaving our current employer and looking for another job.

I went through that downward spiral a few years ago. I had worked for a consulting and training company for eight years in a variety of sales and sales management positions. We had a narrow vertical market in banking, and I was beginning to feel as if I were banging my head against a wall. Clients said that they wanted our help to become better sales organizations, and that doing so was critical to their success. But with scant exceptions, most of them never actually changed anything. Being bankers, doing loans was really what they wanted to do.

I realized that I was burned out, but I hadn't yet thought of leaving the company. I loved the people, and I did have wonderful clients. Then, one day when I was riding the ferry to work, I saw a friend I hadn't seen in a while. She told me about the business she had started and how well she was doing. Her excitement and her passion were so obvious. As I left the ferry and walked to my office, it finally hit me that I had lost excitement for my work. I was bored. I didn't have the drive to develop new business, because I knew it would be the same story all over again.

It was then that I knew I had to leave the company and find another job. I wasn't ready to start my own company, as I didn't have the requisite multi-industry experience. Within two months I had a sales job at another consulting firm. My only limitation was that I was bound by a one-year noncompete agreement, so I couldn't sell to banks. This was perfect: I would now have the opportunity to broaden my capabilities and achieve my goal of multi-industry experience.

I was recharged. The steep learning curve energized me, and I was exposed to a new group of exceptionally bright and engaging people who introduced me to a robust client-interaction process. I learned about business trends and how they impacted my clients, how to question staid thinking, and how to bring in expert resources to support the sale.

Three years later I was ready to start my own company. It was then that I realized I had a choice about how I spent my time. I wanted to spend the least amount of time getting the most results. I wanted to spend it with people I liked and who valued what I brought to the table. Most of all, I wanted to have a good time.

Lots of people say that business is getting tougher, that it's more difficult than ever to sign up new clients—or even to get potential clients to take the time to talk. But the reality is this: It's time to gear up. Real salesmanship is back, returning selling to being the exciting field it was. It's time to unleash that go-get-'em energy we live for. Let's renew the excitement that comes with getting the appointment, having a connected business conversation, and closing deals. Let's focus on the key sales activities that will get us in front of the clients we want to meet.

It is our job as salespeople to *create* opportunities, not wait for them. It's time to reconnect with that super salesperson within us and start making those great deals!

Dollar Value of Referral Selling vs. Cold Calling

In real dollars, compare the results you can expect to get from cold calling versus referral selling. With the industry standard 2 percent response for cold calling, if you spend your time cold calling 150 people, you should be able to set three meetings and convert one of those into a sale. Everybody's situation is different, so you might take a moment to put a dollar value on your typical sale, both in its value to you and, if you're selling for someone else, the value to your company.

Now look at referral selling. Typically, a referred prospect will become a client a minimum 50 percent of the time. If you spend your business-development time on referral-selling activities (following the system explained in this book) and talk to eight people, you should easily generate four meetings—at least two of which will result in a sale. So, at its very basic level, you should be getting double the sales just by switching to referral-selling activities.

Two Surprising Dividends

Dividend One: Referral selling provides you with a way to spend less time and get better results. It provides a better quality of life for *you*.

Spending all day cold calling is unpleasant work and generates a lot of burnout—even from the most seasoned pros. I have never talked to anyone who said they couldn't wait to get into the office to begin their required cold calling for the day. Referral selling, on the other hand, is a delightful person-to-person process, constantly building on achievement and value provided. Referral-selling calls are always productive. You will rarely feel as if you are wasting your time and your life.

Dividend Two: Referral selling begins with trust as a given, so the initial sale is larger, and there is more follow-on business.

A cold-called sale is not based on trust. You may get the sale, but trust will need to be earned over time. A cold-called sale is frequently a trial sale: The customer is waiting to see how you perform. Because a referral sale *begins* as a high-trust relationship sale, the dollar value of a referral sale is typically larger than a cold-called sale. And for a number of reasons, including that a sale begun with trust is more likely to survive any bumps along the delivery road, the follow-on business is generally two to three times that of a sale created by cold calling, and the referred client will become an active Referral Source to others.

Bottom Line: Referral sales are at least double the value of a cold-called sale with half the effort. The quality of your clients and your revenue will increase dramatically. At the same time your cost of sales will decrease, because your salespeople will be spending less time on unproductive business-development activities. This is the essence of what it means to leverage one's time. On an individual basis this understanding can transform anyone from being a novice salesperson to a sales star, and from a sales star into a referral-selling superstar. Implemented company wide, referral selling can transform your enterprise.

You will now experiment with a radically different approach and learn how creating referral sales will result in fewer leads but greatly increased sales. The most exciting challenge you really want to have is finding the time to close all those highly qualified referrals.

Let's examine how you are currently spending your business-development time. Nobody has enough time, so working smarter, not harder, is everyone's goal. There are plenty of metrics around the number of appointments we secure, the number of products we cross-sell, the number of new clients we close, and the revenue we generate from both new and existing clients. But the time we spend on business development is a little more difficult to track. If business development time is measured only by the number of calls you make, you'll be ignoring some considerably more valuable activities.

Business-Development Choices

You engage in a number of activities during your workweek: research, administration, meetings, travel, social engagements, and business development. You need to assess the amount of time you invest each week in business development—what you currently are doing to build relationships that will lead to acquiring new clients or expanding business with existing clients.

Consider the following four categories of business-development activities:

1. **Proactive**—Asking for and getting qualified leads: the time you currently spend asking for and getting qualified referrals
2. **Active**—Creating a presence for your company in the business world and in the community: the time you spend promoting your business brand (e.g., advertis-

ing, mailings, public relations, websites), including
the time you spend responding to inquiries from
these strategies

3. **Personal**—Activities that build your personal visibility and credibility: the time you spend preparing for
and participating in speaking engagements, professional and community groups, conferences, and networking groups—this is the time you spend building
your personal brand

4. **Other**—Other business-development activities you
might be currently doing; for example, cold calling

On the Business-Development Strategy worksheet (see p. 37),
enter the percent of your business-development time (not your
total selling time) that you spend on each category in a typical
week. This is just a guesstimate. Your numbers should total 100
percent. Remember, this is how you're *currently* spending your
business-development time. Complete the form, and then
we'll look at the payoffs.

ACTION STEP 4

Planning Your Time

Complete the Business-Development Strategy worksheet
based on how you are currently spending your time.

Business-Development Strategy

▼

Strategy	Activity	Percent
Proactive	❑ Asking for referrals (asking for and getting qualified leads)	_____ %
Active	❑ Mail campaigns ❑ Marketing leads ❑ Advertising ❑ Responding to inquiries ❑ Trade shows ❑ Internet approaches: Website Listings Groups	_____ %
Personal	❑ Speaking engagements ❑ Professional and community groups ❑ Conferences ❑ Networking and leads groups	_____ %
Other	❑ _____ ❑ _____ ❑ _____ ❑ _____	_____ %
Total		*100%*

How Do I Currently Invest My Time?

Most of your business-development activities are important (except cold calling), but you need to adjust the proportion of time you spend on each based on the payoff you receive. As you adjust the proportion, you will notice far greater results.

Let's examine the significance of each business-development activity.

PROACTIVE

Asking for and getting qualified leads. Most salespeople tell me that they spend between 5 and 20 percent of their business-development time in proactive business development. Your goal is to shift your sales strategy to those activities that will give you the highest payoff. You must create the opportunity, not wait for it. You will then turn those "nice to have" referrals into the way you work all the time, and you will be meeting the people you want to meet.

ACTIVE

Creating a presence for your company in the business world and in the community. Many sales initiatives focus on visibility and credibility. These activities don't make the phone ring off the hook, but they are the necessary underpinnings of a sales strategy and essential to the creation of brand recognition. They include:

Mailing Campaigns

Many sales organizations buy targeted lists and depend on these lists for prospecting activities. Companies that sell lists of sales leads promise that if you use one of their lists, you'll get instant access to the right person in your target company. These companies seem to say that with their lists, you'll learn more about your prospects before you pick up the phone.

But, in fact, lists are not leads. Lists are lists. They may be a way for us to find out who's who in a company and possibly even pinpoint the exact person we are looking for, but they don't guarantee sales.

Our job as salespeople is to *create* business opportunities, not to harbor unrealistic expectations that real leads will be handed to us from a targeted list. "Let's send direct mail or mount an e-mail campaign," we think. "Let's entice people with a free offer. Let's pick up the phone and cold call our list." But that's all just a waste of time and money!

If you want to send a mailing . . . go ahead. But think about how many unsolicited mailings are sent to you that you actually open. In fact, only 38 percent of adults read direct mail based on their current needs, while only 10 percent of adults read all direct mail. And e-mail campaigns have the same poor results. Sales executives tell me that they can easily receive over fifty unsolicited e-mails per day—even with sophisticated spam filters. Hitting the "Delete" button takes even less time than throwing junk mail in the trash.

I'm not against direct mail or e-mail campaigns. I'm against you believing that these initiatives are a way to actively generate new business. They don't. They contribute to your credibility and your branding, and that's it. These approaches are cold. Remember, cold is any marketing approach in which the recipient does not know you and is not expecting to hear from you.

Advertising

Advertising salespeople will be the first to tell you that the purpose of an ad is to get your company's name in front of the public. Period. Please don't run an ad just one or two times. You need at least seven repeat ads and up to twenty for the public to recognize your name. And then a funny thing happens. People will say, "Have you ever heard of No More Cold Calling?" And you say, "I've seen their ads all over the place." The translation you make in your head is that No More Cold Calling must be good, because you recognize the name. Wow, the power of branding!

Trade Shows

To the person—everyone in sales will tell you that leads gotten from trade shows are useless. Trade shows are a "must-attend" for a company's public relations campaigns. The best leads you will get from trade shows are the appointments you make with clients well before they arrive at the venue. And you can frequently get leads from other vendors at the show.

Marketing-Department Leads

Most salespeople rely heavily on their companies' marketing departments to provide them with leads. These leads may come from white papers or targeted mailings they've created. Most are not qualified leads. Salespeople often complain that they're not getting enough leads from marketing. Remember, it's our job to *create* the opportunities, not *wait* for them.

Marketing departments can be effective in crafting compelling messages for salespeople to use or in creating a special offer requesting a customer response. Marketing people, please talk to your sales teams and find out what they need.

PERSONAL

Activities that build personal visibility and credibility. The best thing we can do for ourselves, our customers, and our business is to continue to learn and grow. The more conferences and professional groups we attend, the more we are enriched and the more robust experience and knowledge we bring to our clients. We bring our insights from one client to the next.

Speaking Engagements

Speaking engagements are a perfect venue for you to share your expertise. You will become recognized as the go-to person for your specific skill set. The more times people hear you speak, the more they will recognize your name. This is the best advertisement there is for your personal brand.

I received a call recently from someone who heard me speak over two years ago. She works for a major telecommunications company, and she asked me to speak at an upcoming sales meeting of over one hundred salespeople. You never know who will remember you.

Professional and Community Groups

Professional and community groups are some of the best ways to spread the word. Joining groups is important, but even more important is becoming active in a group. When you volunteer, people learn how you work—you're dependable and contribute innovative ideas—and you begin to develop strong, trusting relationships.

Conferences

Conferences are so numerous today that it's difficult to decide which ones to attend. Find out where your clients and potential clients are going, and then register for those conferences. These are not only phenomenal opportunities to learn and grow, but they also present unparalleled opportunities to be introduced to key decision makers.

Networking Groups

Networking groups are rich business opportunities. Showing up counts. Woody Allen said that 80 percent of success in life is showing up. Network like crazy! Your goal should be to attend at least one event per week at which you'll have an opportunity to meet potential clients. This is a nonnegotiable part of my business-development strategy. You can attend a breakfast, lunch, or evening event—or all three. I have four goals when attending an event: meet interesting people, learn something, get a new client, and have fun. I always achieve at least three of these goals, and I am thrilled!

Decide on groups you would like to join, and show up regularly. Err on the side of joining fewer groups and attending most of the time rather than joining many groups and showing up once in a while. You need to give people the opportunity to get to know you, like you, and trust you.

Leads Groups

Leads groups are a focused and purposeful way to build your business. Typically, these groups are comprised of between twenty and twenty-five people—no one from competing businesses. The concept is to get to know people well enough to feel comfortable referring them. If you join a leads group, please remember that it is not about the members of the group, it's about whom they know. And you don't know the people they know until you ask. Most metropolitan chambers of commerce offer leads groups. Another option is Business Network International (BNI), which has chapters all over the world. Check them out at www.bni.com.

Bottom of the Barrel

Other (including cold calling). You know by now that cold calling just doesn't work. Even though the National Do Not Call Registry only applies to calls from business to consumer, everyone has become wary of cold callers. To date, consumers have registered over 58 million phone numbers, and organizations can be fined up to $11,000 for each infraction. Don't be one of those statistics.

ACTION STEP 5

Leverage Your Time

Meet with your Business Buddy and review the time you spend on business development. Decide which activities are a habit and which you were told to do.

How Am I Committing to Invest My Time in the Future?

Most people are amazed that they are able to shift as much as 30 to 50 percent of their time to high-payoff activities. Many people are shocked to discover that they can sell as much in thirty hours of genuinely satisfying work as they had achieved in the past with a much greater investment of time in grueling, ineffective prospecting.

When you invest in high-payoff sales activities, you are well on your way to becoming a referral-selling star. You will enjoy your work even more, and you will see your business begin to soar.

CHAPTER 4

The World Is Your Sales Team

Wouldn't it be great if you had loads of people out there selling for you and you didn't have to pay them? They would be finding leads for you, putting you in touch with the right people, and maybe even making sales. And in most cases they would be making money for *you*. There are only two ways to get more business: do more business with existing customers or find new customers. What if you could find new customers using a powerful hidden sales team that's already at your disposal? What if all you had to do was flip the "on" switch, and great referrals would just start pouring in?

It's time to think beyond yourself, sales executives, and sales support as your team. There are actually six channels or "teams" that you need to activate to grow your business exponentially.

1. Yourself

Yes, you are your own channel for more business. How well are you activating your referral network? Are you continuing to learn and grow? Are you bringing innovative ideas to your clients? Are you reading books and sharing the content with others? Are you sending books to people you know? Sharing knowledge is powerful.

During the writing of this book, I reconnected with lots of people, and many were curious about the book-writing process. I was visiting one of my colleagues, Bob, on an East Coast trip, and he asked me how much of my methodology I was including in the book. I told him, "Everything." "Aren't you concerned," Bob said, "that people will read the book and won't need your services?" I laughed. I believe that the more we give, the more we get—not just in business, but in our personal lives as well. And no, that's not just a "California thing." I believe that there is a ton of business out there for everyone.

One of my clients, Mark, had sent me a book to read, because the approach was in some ways similar to the work I do. It was a slim book, so I had tucked it into my carry-on bag. I took it out to read on the way home—just two days after my conversation with Bob. Timing is a funny thing. The book, *Love Is the Killer App: How to Win Business and Influence Friends* by Tim Sanders, the chief solutions officer at Yahoo!, suggests giving away information, reading books, sharing with others, creating networks, and forging strong personal connections. I bought dozens of copies to send to my business partners and clients. When you find something wonderful, share it.

2. Other Salespeople

Salespeople know and understand each other. We are the heartbeat of our companies. As salespeople it's our job to bring in the business. We've got good instincts, and we can size people up quickly. We're creative, imaginative, resourceful, and demanding. We're demanding because we want the absolute best for our customers. Without us there would be no company. We're the ones who are always looking for more business and creating any approach in our power to reach or surpass our goals. We'd rather beg for forgiveness than ask for permission.

Even if salespeople don't know each other well, they still have a lot in common. We have similar goals and interesting war stories. We're willing to help each other if at all possible.

WITHIN YOUR COMPANY

Salespeople within your company have huge potential to help you expand your reach. They know people in your territory and in the companies you are targeting. They are also a great resource to tap into to gain more industry knowledge and to discuss account strategies.

One of my clients has strong incentives for its salespeople to refer their clients to other salespeople in the company. If the referral results in a sale, the referring salesperson gets a percent of the commission. The company has not only been able to instill a culture that supports referrals, but also one in which people are always looking for opportunities to refer business to their buddies.

OUTSIDE OF YOUR COMPANY

There are salespeople outside of your company who are in aligned fields.

A client of mine gave me an example from her company—I'll call it Datastor—which provides data storage-management systems for large enterprises. For a Datastor salesperson, complementary relationships with salespeople at corresponding hardware companies such as disk array companies, tape drive companies, or companies that manufacture storage switches are smart alliances. They also look for cooperative arrangements with software and services companies that develop storage tools, database software, or systems integrators.

Having some or all of these relationships in place helps a Datastor salesperson better manage a client's storage environment, and the salesperson becomes valued as a consultative resource.

YOUR COMPETITORS

Salespeople who are your competitors may not have the breadth or depth of resources to service the client. Their solutions may not be scalable, or their organization may be at capacity. Their product may not always be as good a fit as yours for some customers, and they will increase their own credibility by occasionally recommending your solution.

Granted, you may not be the first to raise your hand to refer a competitor. However, there are industries that regularly refer business to each other. One example is a staffing company that specializes in administrative placement. Perhaps a client asks them to find an individual who is outside of their realm—say a financial analyst. One staffing company will work out an arrangement with another staffing company if they don't have the right candidate, because their only goal is to find the best person for the client. Training companies regularly refer business to each other. One company may specialize in sales, while another focuses on customer service or leadership development.

If we really care about our clients, then we will dedicate ourselves to finding the best solutions for them. We become Referral Resources, and one of the greatest things we can do for our clients—and for our reputations—is to be trusted and valued Referral Resources.

3. Employees

The fact is, the best resource for potential new business is all around you. Everyone in your organization knows dozens and maybe even hundreds of other people. Now who do you think understands the value of your organization better than the people who work there? And who could possibly have more invested in your company's success? Your job will be to bring everyone in your company into the sales process. Start by finding out whom they know. To do that, you need to help everyone in your organization understand that they are part of the sales team—whether they have an official sales title or not.

I learned a major lesson about how to activate a powerful network within the normal, everyday connections people have. One day I was in the coffee room of the consulting firm where

I worked, talking to one of my counterparts about the difficulty I was having connecting with the VP of sales at a high-tech company. A rather new IT employee overheard my conversation and said he thought he could help. "Oh sure," I thought. "He's just an IT guy." It turns out that his mother was the executive assistant for the sales VP at the company I was trying to reach. And help she did. She made the introduction, and I got the appointment. With that, I learned never to prejudge people or the contributions they can make to the sales effort.

Where did your fellow employees work before they came to your company? Who are their next-door neighbors? Who are their family members who work at your prospect companies? Take the time to talk to them; learn about their history and what is important. Help them to understand that with every sale, the company prospers, and their jobs become more secure.

4. Distributors

Getting others to sell your products often extends your reach without costing you additional overhead. The challenge, however, is mindshare. How do you ensure that your distribution partners recommend your product over your competitor's and remain loyal to you over time? Success with your distribution-channel sellers requires that you spend a fair amount of time giving them the product and selling information they need to represent you well.

Generally, you only have a few opportunities to get your distributors excited about your products. Therefore, the proper care and feeding of distributors is essential. Your distributors will then have the tools and techniques to increase their sales, and you will gain a competitive edge over hundreds of other suppliers.

> *If you'd like to learn how to get the most out of your distributors, I'd like to refer you to Jeff Grover at www.grovergroupllp.com and ask about his program, Driving Distributor Demand. The Grover Group will create a customized, product-focused, interactive learning experience, which will teach your salespeople the questions to ask to uncover needs and address customer problems.*

5. Alliances

Business today is driven by the overwhelming pressure to cut the cost of sales, so creating strategic alliances is a way of selling that's on a major upswing. There are two types of strategic alliances—those made by organizations and those made by salespeople.

ORGANIZATIONS

By sharing resources, organizations can merge their product offerings or even create new products jointly, enabling everyone involved to penetrate markets faster while reducing risks and costs. Strategic sales alliances have the power to create intimacy, loyalty, and a built-in referral network that can quickly become immune to the pressure of the competition.

SALESPEOPLE

Salespeople who have built powerful alliances know whom to call on. They can set up meetings quickly and can dramatically shorten the sales cycle. They will receive leads that they otherwise wouldn't have had access to, and they will reach the decision makers faster because of their increased credibility. These salespeople are the ones most likely to be identified as trusted business partners.

Even if a corporate sales or marketing organization has not set up formal cross-selling relationships with complementary product or service companies, it behooves the salespeople to determine who those players might be and to initiate local relationships. A formal relationship might include co-marketing efforts, formal lead sharing and registration, and even referral fees of some kind. Even without this structure, savvy salespeople can evaluate the market landscape, determine who might be the best partners, and contact their counterparts to initiate relationships.

Developing Your Strategic Alliances

There are several opportunities for you to create strategic alliances.

- Identify organizations that call on the same customer as you but offer a different product or solution. If you are selling interviewing training techniques, anyone else selling to a VP of human resources would be a potential strategic partner.
- Determine the types of businesses that provide services to your customer, either above or below you in the supply chain. As an example, a company that sells CRM solutions might form a strategic alliance with a sales

training company as well as a sales consulting organization in order to offer a complete solution to its clients.

• Look for companies that have a foothold in different markets than you do—perhaps a vertical market that you don't address, or an international market that you would like to be sold in. As salespeople, we know that issues from one company to the next are pretty much the same, but all customers think theirs are unique. Alliances can provide your customers with an adequate comfort level about your experience in their industry as well as your global capabilities. Alliances can be project based or more strategic company-to-company agreements.

I was working with a Bay Area public relations firm that had exceptional expertise and a formidable track record in high tech. Its one drawback was that it had limited experience globally. It knew that in responding to a particular request for proposal, the only way it would have a chance of winning would be to demonstrate to the client that it could deliver globally. The firm decided to form an alliance with a global PR firm that would be its delivery arm. It negotiated a formal agreement for this one project.

Think about what you need to win a deal. Ask yourself the following questions before entering into a strategic alliance:

• Is it real? The company that put out the RFP is serious about implementing your solution. You have commitment from key stakeholders. You have iden-

tified the decision maker and know that there is a
budget.
- Can I win? You know the competition and are confident that you have a viable position. You've been given
access to key people in the decision-making process.
- Is it worth it? Determine whether the time and resources you put into winning the deal will advance
your position in the marketplace and bring you increased revenue and profits. Will this alliance make
the difference in your getting the deal?

Don't enter a strategic alliance thinking that it will last forever. Your alliance may be solution- or project-focused, and
then you will need to move on. However, if a strategic alliance
can help you win a contract and it's worth the considerable
extra effort—go for it!

ACTION STEP 6

Build Your De Facto Sales Team

1. Meet with a sales executive you know in a different industry. Find out how he is managing strategic alliances. Identify
   a company that could be an alliance partner for you.
2. Determine who is above and below you in your supply
   chain, and identify potential partners.
3. Meet with a potential partner and explore opportunities. Probe for common values.

6. Your Affinity Network

Now I want you to consider another channel—the cultural, geographic, and special interest connections you have that can lead to new business. This is your Affinity Network. Think about people you know who are of the same cultural or religious background as you, or even people from the same geographic region or country. What about others who share the same political agenda as you or your passion for travel or sports? Don't you feel an immediate connection with them—a natural liking or inclination, or a feeling of identification?

Think of a Brit working for a company in the United States. The company has a major business opportunity in the United Kingdom. Who is it going to send? Given the choice, it's not going to be someone from Texas or New York. The company is going to send the Brit, because he will be perceived by the potential client as "one of them."

Even within the United States, people have geographic affinities. Years ago, I was traveling with one of my sales reps to Little Rock, Arkansas. We had a meeting with a senior VP of one of the major banks in town. I was the senior person on the call in my role as sales manager from San Francisco, and Jon was a salesman from Chicago. The client had grown up in the Midwest, and she immediately identified with my salesman as a fellow Midwesterner. I was, apparently, from a place so far away culturally (San Francisco) that I was beyond understanding. The two of them shared an immediate connection—common values, similar thinking, instant trust. The buyer never even addressed me. I'm convinced that we made the sale, in part, because of their regional affiliation.

I taught a workshop to the Asia-Pacific group of a large organization. As a facilitator, I needed to know the cultural nuances regarding building relationships and referrals. That part wasn't difficult to discover; I simply asked the client to give me some background. My biggest challenge was to be able to make an immediate connection with the group. Wanting to bridge our cultural gap, I began by telling them that I was fortunate enough to have made a trip to China a few months before and that I had learned two words in Mandarin—"hello" and "thank you." I recited those two words, and they all laughed and said that my accent was really good. We connected immediately.

Travel is one of the greatest connectors. No matter what your nationality, if you are traveling in a foreign country, you immediately gravitate to people from home. Sometimes you even become friends with those people for life. And when you're doing business and you let clients know about a recent or upcoming vacation, you have something exciting to discuss. (They wish that they were going, too.) Travel is still intriguing and exotic.

One of my hobbies is hiking. I've joined different hiking groups, and even though I knew no one at the start, I had made some good acquaintances by the end. I wouldn't have talked to these "strangers" if I had met them on the street, but there was an immediate acceptance and trust between us when we discovered that we had the same hobby.

And what about sports? That's not just a guy thing. No, I

don't need to know who played third base for the Pittsburgh Pirates in 1960 (Don Hoak), but it does help when people know I'm from San Francisco and that I love the Giants. Before I visit a client in any city, I find out how its professional sports team is doing. We can exult if it is doing well and commiserate if it is doing poorly.

You get the picture: If you can establish a common interest, the connection is immediate, and it's significant. The faster you can tap into the various connections you have, the faster you or someone in alliance with you will become accepted and trusted by your targeted client group. Your allies will become a powerful source of referrals for you.

Yourself, other salespeople, employees, distributors, alliances, networks—these are the opportunities you can leverage to propel your business.

ACTION STEP 7

Explore Options

- Identify one person you know in each category who might help you to grow your business.
- Schedule a time to meet with these people to exchange ideas and explore options for working together.

To build your extended sales team, you will constantly be talking to people with an ear to how extensive their contacts might be. You should always be collecting information about these contacts. You will uncover interesting facts and identify potential opportunities in the most unusual places. I guarantee it. You'll regularly find out who others know and tap into their networks. You will have a reward and recognition system in place that actively supports referral generation. You'll be working with others who realize and understand the exponential power of sharing resources and sharing knowledge. All of you will become more powerful.

You will then have others "paying you"—they will be selling your services and will be giving you perfect referrals. You will have a de facto sales team that will knock out your competition and drive your business forward with amazing velocity. Your company will quickly build momentum, and others will not be able to keep pace. Your revenue and profits will soar, and you really will leave your competition in the dust.

CHAPTER 5

Follow the Yellow Brick Road

You've made the decision to shift to referral selling and to enroll others in your referral-selling approach. Your momentum is building, and you've decided to include as many people as possible on your sales team. It's now time to align your organization and make it referral-selling ready.

To ensure your success in shifting to referral selling, you will need a clearly defined sales process. A sales process is like a road map. The members of your team will be able to agree on the signposts and know where they are going. They will know when to bring in additional resources, where they have competitive superiority, and where and when they have opportunities to ask for referrals.

The sales process really has just two steps:

- **Step One:** Getting in front of the right people
- **Step Two:** Everything that happens after that.

This may sound glib, but think about it. We've talked about the importance of getting in front of the right people and how that one activity alone—being referred—dramatically collapses the sales process, elevates you above the competition, creates trust, and guarantees a new customer over 50 percent of the time.

There's been way too much attention paid to the balance of the sales process: conducting a meeting, developing questioning skills, overcoming objections, closing—blah, blah, blah. Yes, we do need to know how to listen and how to question, how to create a sense of urgency, and how to advance the sale. But if we're not in front of the right person to begin with, it really doesn't matter. That being said, let's look at the entire sales process.

Mapping Your Sales Process

You may think that everyone knows and understands their company's sales process, but there are frequently different interpretations—especially with a distributed sales force. If you do not have a written sales process, now is the time to create one. Your process will keep you anchored to referral-based business-development activities.

During our consulting work with clients, we discuss and get agreement on each step of the company's sales process. We then ask our clients what occurs *between* each step. Surprisingly, the activities that take place between the big steps are frequently the hidden steps that are critical to winning new business.

As an example, when you've been referred, how can you

find out more about the client's business? That research is a step. What do you do after an initial meeting? That follow-up is a step. What is your strategy for winning this account? Who will be on the engagement team? What additional information do you need to write a proposal? Who will be the lead presenter? Every action you take should advance the sale. Otherwise, why do it? Once you've mapped your primary steps, you'll always find many more critical steps in between. When you're finished, you've captured *all* the steps for a complete process that others can follow.

There are opportunities for referral activities in each part of the sales process and opportunities to involve many other resources within and outside of your company. As you map your sales process, you'll also be looking at the unique activities that must take place for referral selling to come alive and be self-sustaining.

A typical sales process includes the following steps:

1. Lead Generation (Prospecting)

This step begins with the development of a tightly crafted prospecting strategy. Include only those activities that will attract your best customers in the shortest time frame. Your most important action is to set a goal for the number of people you will ask for referrals every week and the number of referral meetings you will schedule every week.

One of my clients told me that his sales team had a problem closing deals. They got appointments easily, but they weren't converting appointments into sales. Their conversion rate was dismal—less than 20 percent. He thought they needed training on closing skills. I thought they needed to redirect their prospecting activities and learn how to get better appointments. By focusing on the qualifications of their Ideal Customer and getting referred to the right person, my client's team was able to increase their close ratio by more than 20 percent. Additionally, they freed up scarce, expensive technical resources that had gotten bogged down in the prospecting process.

Prospecting Traps to Avoid

We often engage in sales activities that waste time and slow down the sales process. We get meetings for the sake of getting meetings, and then get frustrated because there is no interest or we can't seem to advance the sale. We call to follow up, and no one calls us back. We forecast business that isn't real, and we get reprimanded by management for not meeting our goals. Managers count on our projections to make their projections, so their ability to deliver is questioned.

We keep this ridiculous cycle going because we are expected to generate a certain number of appointments. I spoke to a client recently who was perfectly honest with me. He said that he agreed with my process and knew that he could be successful at referral selling, but that wasn't how he was measured by his manager. He was measured on the number of calls he made. Aha! Referral selling will never be the way you work if you are measured by the number of calls you make.

Measure Prospecting Activities

Whether you are a CEO, VP of sales, sales manager, or

salesperson, you need to determine the essential referral-selling metrics in the prospecting stage of your sales process. Not later. Now! If you are a sales executive, set referral-prospecting metrics for your team. If you are a salesperson, set your own metrics, or work with your Business Buddy. Don't count on management to set your course. They will guide you, but ultimately, you must be accountable for the results of your lead-generation activities.

Typical prospecting-referral metrics to consider are:

1. The number of people you will ask for referrals each week
2. The number of referrals you receive that match your Ideal Customer
3. The number of meetings you have with your referred prospects
4. The number of referred prospects who become customers
5. The length of time it takes to convert a referred prospect into a customer
6. The average dollar value of a referred customer vs. your average sale

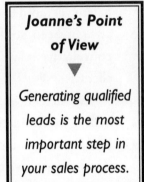

Joanne's Point of View

▼

Generating qualified leads is the most important step in your sales process.

2. PLAN AND CONDUCT MEETINGS

You've received a referral, and now you are meeting in person to more completely understand the prospect's business issues, values, and goals. Because you've been referred, you've already eliminated those first uncomfortable steps in the sales process—how to begin the conversation and how to establish trust and credibility.

I had a breakfast meeting with a prospect (VP) who had been referred to me. Within a very few minutes he disclosed a fair amount of confidential information about his organization, which he wouldn't have done unless I'd been referred. In fact, he told me he was sharing this information with me because we were "already friends." It was a remarkable demonstration of the power of a referred prospect.

In referral selling your initial meetings can be radically different from what you've been used to. In referral selling the initial meeting is usually the time to jump right in and ask insightful questions. Then be ready to listen intently to the answers. You are going to get much more information than you have ever gotten in a first meeting before, because you've already been sold. Now's the time to begin a productive consultative relationship and start solving problems for your client.

By the end of your initial meeting, you should be able to make a determination as to whether this opportunity is viable. You should also understand the client's decision-making process, whether you have competition, and the specs for submitting a proposal.

You will have many additional meetings within the organization in order to collect data, enhance your value proposition, and get buy-in for your initiative. Each subsequent meeting should be planned and strategic.

3. Proposal

It's now time to write your proposal—if one is necessary. Many clients must request a proposal because it's company policy. You clearly have the advantage because you've been referred. You have insider knowledge, and in most cases your client will tell you what to include in the proposal. You must clearly identify the customer's current situation, the benefits of your solution, the anticipated results, your project plan or time line, and the costs. Be absolutely clear about what your services do and do not cover and for how long your price quote is good. Pricing is a funny thing. It's the customer's job to push back on price, and it's your job to demonstrate value. Don't make any assumptions. Here's a caveat I have in my proposals: *Prices are based on the scope of the project as outlined in this proposal. All quoted prices are in effect for sixty (60) days.* This statement alone will help prevent "scope creep" and will protect you if prices need to increase.

4. Presentation

Find out from your Referral Source all the people who will be present—what their roles are and what concerns they have—and reconfirm the decision-making process. If you are one of several vendors presenting, determine where you are in the order. If you have a choice, go first or last.

There are different schools of thought on the preferred order. If you go first, you can set the criteria for how others will be evaluated. You can even provide a checklist for each attendee to use. The topics on the checklist will be derived from your conversations with the company and what you know is critical, i.e., team is flexible, meets tight deadlines, has geographic reach, offers creative ideas, is competent; solution is scalable.

If you go last, you have the opportunity to find out what is important for the group to hear. What did they hear that they liked, and what haven't they heard? You can also present a choice of topics and see what they would like to discuss first. And of course, you should have a very strong close and ask for the business at the end.

5. CLOSE

If you've taken all the right steps, covered your bases, and created a compelling business case, the client's decision will be a no-brainer. Closing should be as simple as putting one foot in front of the other.

When you've been referred, the client often closes for you. Think of meetings you've attended where your Referral Source has introduced you (with a strong bias), and before the end of the meeting, the attendees were exploring options about ways to work together. Ultimately, if you have problems closing, you need to revisit the earlier steps in the sales process. Difficulty in closing always indicates that something earlier was overlooked, forgotten, or not addressed.

6. IMPLEMENT

The challenge is always in the implementation. The client's road may be paved with good intentions, but many initiatives never gather momentum. Aristotle said, "Well begun is half done." There are many moving parts—not just in your product or service, but with all the people at your client's company. Your engagement team will work together with various stakeholders—some with frequent interaction and some with limited interaction. You'll be meeting people who may not have been involved in the sale. They may be thrilled that you are there, or they may resent your presence.

The key to smoothing the road and ensuring the success of any project is having a strong project team and project manager and clear client expectations. Be sure to have an internal launch meeting in which you get your team together, brief them on the project and the clients, and outline clear roles and responsibilities, time lines, and deliverables. When you have your actual launch meeting with the client, ask the client how they would like to work and how they would like to communicate. We often focus too heavily on what we are going to do and not on how we are going to work together with the client.

You need to know how the client will know when the project is successful. One of my clients was a senior line manager. Early in the implementation I asked him to give me his view of what success would look like. Referral business was currently 10 percent of their revenue, and he wanted to double that amount. We agreed to begin the implementation in one region and decided on a ninety-day period to generate proof of success. At the end of that time, or once the success criteria were met, we would expand our work into other regions.

Be sure to set specific, measurable success criteria so that you can check in with the client at appropriate milestones as well as at the end of the project. Because you will be asking for referrals when success is assured, you want to lay the groundwork for the client's definition of success now.

7. Penetrate Account/Obtain Referrals

Your project team is on the ground and in place to ask for referrals. They are doing the work and have day-to-day contact with the client. The challenge is that they do not see themselves as salespeople. If you've done your homework and enrolled them in the referral process, they will understand that their role is to ask for referrals and get an introduction to other buying centers in the organization. You will take over from there. Most of the time your implementation people will be very willing to make the introduction. They just don't want any part of the rest of the process—that "salesy" stuff.

During the sales process and presentation, you and others from your company will meet many people in the client organization. If you bring in senior people, they will likely make connections with their peers. You will have your own contacts. It is up to all of you to ask for referrals. Remember, you don't have to wait until the project is complete. You can ask at any point after you've delivered value to the client—after you've suggested an alternative that will save them time and money, accelerated the time line, introduced them to a valuable resource, or told the truth when it was tough to do.

Here is a typical sales process (see p. 69). See how what you do compares.

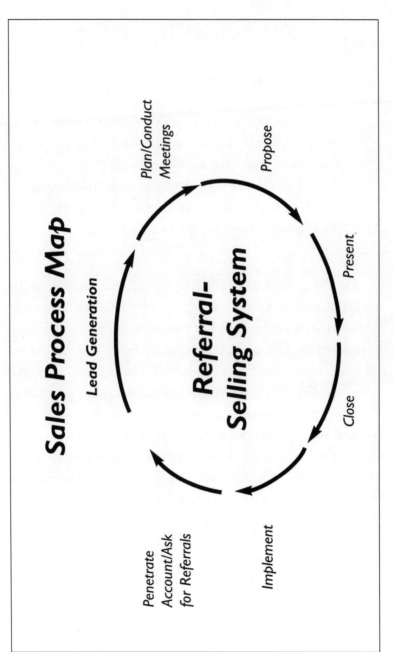

ACTION STEP 8

Map Your Proprietary Sales Process

- On the worksheet Your Sales Process (see p. 71), identify the main stages in your sales process and the activities or tasks that occur at each stage.
- Work with your Business Buddy to complete the map.
- Identify opportunities to ask for referrals, and integrate the essential referral activities into each stage.

Databases such as ACT!, GoldMine, and Salesforce.com are CRM tools to help us execute our sales process. They compile our customer data and can track where we are in the sales process. In ACT! you can customize the fields, but the generic ones are Initial Communication, Needs Assessment, Presentation, Negotiation, Commitment to Buy, and Sales Fulfillment. Your biggest challenge will not be in creating your sales process. Your biggest challenge will be in the implementation. It is easy to be drawn backward into the way you used to work. You must now make lead generation a priority, and referral activities must occur each and every day.

Your Sales Process ▼	
Step	**Steps In Between**
1	
2	
3	
4	
5	
6	
7	

ACTION STEP 9

Review Your Database

Customize the sales process fields in your database to match your proprietary sales process.

Now that you've mapped your sales process, the next step is to determine your success measures. How will you know when you've been successful in using a referral-selling process? Set monthly, quarterly, and yearly goals for the number of new clients you want to attract, the additional business you want to get with existing clients, the increase in profits you want to see, or the number of new relationships you want to make.

ACTION STEP 10

Set Your Referral Goals

- Meet with your Business Buddy and determine your success measures.
- Keep your sales process handy, refer to it often, and don't forget to ask for referrals.

Referrals are immediate and can be the key to quickly increasing revenue and profits. Referral-lead generation produces the results that the bank, the shareholders, you (the sales force), and the CEO love. Referral development is the most active and personal stage of business development. Although referral selling is the fastest and most cost-effective way to get new clients, referral generation requires the most discipline and dedication.

When an organization is shifting to referral selling, it must abandon throwing resources chaotically into various lead-generation avenues and make the shift to coordinating its branding activities with referral-driven client-creation efforts. Every company faces choices about how to spend its lead-generation money and resources. The most cost-effective and efficient resource is a salesperson operating a referral-based business.

Whether you are an individual salesperson or a company of salespeople, success in referral selling means integrating referral activities into the way you work every day. If your plan is to shift to referral selling, it means knowing and following your current sales process and then determining the referral activities that occur in each phase.

Referrals don't just happen. If you are going to dramatically increase your revenue, profits, and relationships—and also have more free time—you must make them happen. You can't assume that existing customers will automatically take the initiative to make referrals just because salespeople or their companies have done good work. Nor will you be able to exult any longer in those occasional referral phone calls you receive.

You will need to take specific steps to hard wire referrals into the way you work.

You'll not only get to the Emerald City, but you'll find you won't need a wizard, because you had what it takes all along.

CHAPTER 6

Tick, Tick, Tick: You Have Ten Seconds to Get a Smile

There's a saying among salespeople that customers buy with emotion and justify with fact. If our customers don't like us or don't feel comfortable with us, they won't buy from us. You might believe that over the long term people will grow to like you because they will find out that you're honest and reliable about following up and that you remember your customers' birthdays and so on. But the reality is that you need people to start liking you within the first ten seconds of your relationship. That's really all you have to get off on the right foot. Ten seconds.

Connect with people, and you will have the business. If you connect with the business problem only and don't take the time to relate one-on-one with your client, you won't have the client, and you won't have the sale. I tell my clients that business is serious, but people aren't.

I don't believe in using tired sales techniques like walking into someone's office and commenting on the photographs and awards. This is outdated and transparently insincere. When we are referred, we have an immediate connection. We talk about the person who referred us and discard those first uncomfortable and awkward steps of the sales process—explaining who we are and what we do. We also discard the question we always wrestle with: How am I going to begin the conversation? There is significant research about why clients make buying decisions. Bottom line: It's because they *like* and *trust* the salesperson and her organization.

When I worked at a prominent consulting firm, we had a formal process for following up with prospective clients. Whether we won or lost a piece of business, I could ask an executive at my firm who was not involved in the sales process to contact the client and find out the reasons why the client decided to work with us—or not. We already felt strongly that we were offering the right solution—otherwise we wouldn't have been at the table in the first place. Additionally, our prospective clients knew that we would deliver on time and within budget. It turned out that the deciding factor was whether or not they liked us. That's the simple truth: Clients make multimillion dollar decisions because they like us.

According to Susan RoAne (www.susanroane.com), recent research at both Harvard and Stanford universities reveals that the number-one skill for success in the twenty-first century is the ability to talk to other people. If we don't connect with others, there is really no next step: no referrals, no job offers, no promotions, no alliances. In the first ten seconds you have to intrigue people enough that they will say, "Tell me more."

The only goal of your initial interaction is to have the next interaction. Period. The first thing out of your mouth cannot be your company's party line, the specs of your latest device, or a ten-point comparison of your product with the competition's. You need to immediately connect on an intimate, personal level, and unless you do that, you won't have earned the right to have a second interaction.

We're asked to explain what we do all the time—at business meetings, networking events, parties, weddings, reunions, on airplanes—every place. Think of ways you can introduce yourself and position your business so that you will always make a human connection.

"So, what do you do?" Too often, we respond with "corporate speak." We blurt out phrases like, "I sell software," "I work for a staffing company," "I'm an attorney," "I'm a writer," or "I'm an accountant." Our immediate reflex is to tell people our true profession. This is what we've been taught, and we've never considered any other response, unless you sell insurance. Insurance salespeople already know that starting off by saying what they do is the fastest way to clear a room.

Think about the times you've been bored to tears when people told you what they did for a living. Can't you still see them, rambling on and on about their work while you couldn't have cared less? You've probably heard of the thirty-second commercials people use in business groups. You may even have perfected one yourself. The fact is, you don't have thirty seconds to explain yourself when you meet someone. Get a timer and set it for thirty seconds. Now let it run, and just wait until it's finished. I do this all the time in my workshops, and the participants are amazed at how long it is. Now set your timer for ten seconds. You'll discover that ten seconds is plenty of time for your introduction.

Let's learn a way to introduce yourself that will absolutely intrigue the other person. I want you to be able to "connect" with almost anyone with the first words out of your mouth. How will you know when it's working? Well, the other person may smile, laugh, ask you a question, or say, "Tell me more." Gone forever will be the blank stares, uncomfortable interactions, or people leaving the room.

Your message should be succinct, compelling, and have a hook. A hook will cause someone to say, "Really? Tell me more," or "That sounds really interesting," or "How do you do that?"

Introducing yourself in ten seconds or less can be one of the most challenging things you will ever learn to do. Most salespeople can talk about their business for hours, but crystallizing what they do in a couple of sentences and then stopping takes discipline. You will need to develop two or three compelling introductions and then test them with your Business Buddy. When you get a positive response, that's a keeper. Your goal is to develop several dynamite introductions that are fresh, interesting, and intriguing.

When I introduce myself in ten seconds at a networking event, my only goal is to make people smile—that's the ultimate connection in any language. If someone smiles, I know that we've connected. Smiling is one of those involuntary physical reactions that just happens. Sometimes when I'm walking down the street, I notice that everyone coming toward me is smiling. I'm thinking to myself, "I don't know these people, so why are they smiling at me?" Then I realize that I have a smile on my face. So, when you're at your next networking event, smile at people when you shake hands. They will smile back. Try it. It's magic.

Here is an example of an introduction that needed some work. This was from an IT professional *after* he had the background information that I just gave to you. "I help companies maximize their ROI on strategic IT and product initiatives through financial planning modeling and logical system modeling." Do you think that would get a lot of smiles?

I asked my IT client to put down his paper and just tell me in his own words what he loved best about his job. Without thinking for more than a few seconds, he gave me this answer: "I help people solve tough problems in tough times." Wow! Wouldn't you want to know more? Everyone in the room cheered and applauded. I told him that when he went to his next networking event, he should put "Tough Guy" on his name tag. You can bet he got a lot of interesting questions.

My name tag says the name of my company—No More Cold Calling. When people ask what I do, I tell them that I'm the Referral Queen. I always get laughs and a jumpstarted conversation.

Here are some more examples of hooks to read before you start working on crafting your own:

Health Insurance: I make body maintenance affordable.
Attorney: I help clients win the game of jury lotto; OR I make sure you're not lost in the fine print.

Alarm Company: I'm an alarmist.

Caterer: I cater to the needs of party animals.

Corporate Hotel Sales: I tuck people in at night.

Paper Products: I sell toilet paper.

Office Systems: I bring people from the dark ages to the digital age.

Mobile Phones: I put technology into phones to save lives.

Staffing Company: I keep people off the streets; OR I'm a fairy *job*mother.

Big-Four Firm: I'm your Final Four pick; OR I keep you out of the headlines in the *Wall Street Journal.*

Meeting Planner: I relieve stress better than a martini.

Banker: I'm the banker you wish you had; OR I work with dead presidents.

Architect: I make sure you're not lost in space.

Orthodontist: I brace people for success.

CPA: I am Tylenol for new business headaches; OR I take the *lie* out of *compliance.*

Technical Recruiter: I rob banks (pause) of their greatest asset—people.

Metropolitan Chamber: I play connect the dots all day.

Advertising Sales: I help companies expose themselves and not get caught with their pants down.

Auto Body Company: We always meet by accident.

Marble Company (countertops): We're counter-fitters with counter intelligence.

Mortgage Broker: I help people find money in places they wouldn't think to look.

Cosmetic Dentist: We have a frequent smile program.
Travel Agent: I tell people where to go.

Your first reaction to these introductions might be that they are too cute. I have heard that objection before. None of these introductions is off-color or offensive. There's a difference between being clever and being cute. People appreciate clever. Whether you are a CEO, VP of sales, sales manager, or salesperson, you need a compelling introduction. You may think that because you're an executive, introductions don't matter. I say that if what you're doing is working, keep doing it. If you're meeting the people you need to meet and are getting the next meeting, there's no need to change. If not, try something new, and remember that clever is welcome in any situation—business or social. You can use your new introduction anyplace.

Now it's time to try some of your own introductions. Here is a worksheet to help you trigger some thoughts.

But first, write down your current reply when someone asks you what you do: _____

_____

Now take a few minutes and review the statements posed on the worksheet (see pp. 83–4) and write down what first comes to mind.

- *What's the most unusual aspect of what you do?*
    Think about several client examples and the results you delivered.

What do you do in your work that others don't
know about?

- *Most interesting?*
  What client story would leave your listener spell-
  bound?

- *Most exciting?*
  When was a contract or deliverable down to the
  wire?
  When did you have to fill in for someone on your
  team?

- *Most dramatic?*
  Tell us about a presentation you made that
  knocked the client's socks off.
  When did you mobilize a global team in record
  time?

- *Most humorous?*
  How do you make your clients laugh?
  When do you have the best time?

Write down some thoughts that come to you immediately.
Above all, ask yourself what you love most about what you do,
and think about the results you consistently deliver.

Tick, Tick, Tick—
You Have Ten Seconds to Get a Smile

▼

	How Do I Differentiate Myself?
Criteria ❏ Succinct ❏ Compelling ❏ Has a hook	Most unusual aspect of what I do
	Most interesting aspect of what I do
	Most exciting aspect of what I do
	Most dramatic aspect of what I do
	Most humorous aspect of what I do
	My Ten-Second Introductions
Remember *It's all about customers— not about you!* *Talk about the results you deliver.*	

ACTION STEP 11

Create Your Ten-Second Introduction

- Get together with a friend or your Business Buddy and test your introduction.
- Attend a networking event and introduce yourself with your new message.

You Got That Smile, Now Deliver on the Promise

OK, so you've piqued someone's interest, and the person says, "Tell me more," or "How do you do that?" Now what do you do? You have two options, and they both need to be short. Your goal for this second interaction is to determine if there is enough interest on both sides for you to schedule a face-to-face meeting.

1. Ask a question. Yes, you can answer a question with a question. Think about how what you do will resonate with someone. What is a common experience that most people in corporations face? When you tap into a personal experience, you will continue to build your connection. The other person will then begin to talk about her situation, and you are now in a conversation.

I ask some of the following questions:

"Have you ever been in a situation when you had a quota to meet and you weren't able to get enough appointments to present your solution?"

"Have you ever worked with really difficult clients?"

"Has prospecting for leads worn you down?"

People can relate to these situations immediately, and they start telling me horror stories. I can then discuss the work we do and how we can prevent these situations from recurring. We've not only connected, but we've quickly identified opportunities to work together. I couldn't ask for a better scenario.

Want to learn more about how to be great at networking? Read Susan RoAne's books How to Work a Room *and* The Secrets of Savvy Networking. *Susan is the networking maven. Check her out at www.susanroane.com.*

---

2. Tell a story about one of your clients and keep it to thirty seconds. People will pay more attention to a story than to your bragging about what you do. Here is the best way to tell a story: State the *situation*, describe the *action* you took, and then articulate the *results* you achieved.

Here's my example: One of my clients had an experienced, commissioned sales force that had been dramatically impacted by the economic downturn. They had a drastic reduction in clients, and their incomes had been cut in half. As a result of teaching them my referral-selling system and delivering some follow-up coaching, the remaining sales force of only eight people generated 102 referrals in six weeks and closed twenty new deals in six months, which put them up 30 percent over the previous year!

Your challenge will be *not* using your old, boring introduction. You will be tempted to fall back into your old ways.

I'm asking you to try something new—to do something different than you've been doing for your entire career. Be passionate, and your excitement will be contagious. I can guarantee you that when you use your new introduction, you will have a great time and will be a huge success in your networking activities and your ability to connect.

Do you have a great introduction? Terrific. Send an e-mail to me at joanne@nomorecoldcalling.com and let me know what it is. You need more than one, so get cranking and develop a repertoire of three or four dynamite intros.

The goal of each interaction is to earn the right to have the next interaction. Period. You'll know that you've hit a home run if someone says to you, "Tell me more."

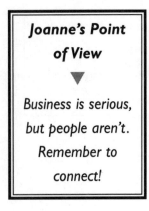

Joanne's Point of View

▼

Business is serious, but people aren't. Remember to connect!

CHAPTER 7

All the Wrong Places

Imagine that you're single and looking for a long-term relationship. You're wiser now than you used to be, so you take the time to reflect a little and decide to make a profile of your perfect mate. It turns out you want someone who is sober, smart, hardworking, honest, and loves theater and concerts. Now, would you go looking for that person in a bar?

How is it we end up with a few customers that just drive us crazy? I call those customers PITAs, or "pain in the ass" customers. PITA customers are never happy, and the red flags are commonplace: PITA customers don't return calls, they batter salespeople on price, and they make unreasonable demands. In short, they're draining, using up valuable resources in the organization. Have too many PITA customers and before long, profits will dwindle. That's not a compelling scenario. Yet companies continue to accept this bad business, all the while thinking it's better than no business. But is it?

When organizations take bad business, it creates an opportunity cost, because serving a PITA customer takes away

scarce resources that could have been used to go after the phenomenal clients they want and need to make money.

When you move over to referral selling, you need to be
even more careful of the company you keep.

The PITA Price Downward Spiral

There's only one thing worse than a PITA customer, and that's
a PITA customer you get by cutting your price. In the world
of referral selling, you will have launched yourself into a downward spiral.

If price is the only decision point for a client, the red flags
should be waving so furiously that you turn around and run
the other way as quickly as possible. Someone is trying to turn
you into a commodity, and a nickel-and-dime approach is just
the beginning. You will be squeezed on everything and expected to deliver additional services at no charge.

Marketing people will tell you that 95 percent of salespeople compromise on price before their customer has even
brought it up. The fact is that customers are willing to pay
more if they receive exceptional service, if the service translates
into increased revenue and profits, if time to market is decreased, if a company anticipates their needs, if the sales team
is easy to work with, and if the company can demonstrate
proven results.

I believe that we get what we pay for. There's always going
to be a trade-off between best, fast, and cheap. You can only
pick two. Arlene is a leading salesperson in her company. She

once had a customer I'll call Jane. Jane was a senior VP with a premier global company who let it be known that she always brought in the best resources to work with her executives. She flew in renowned speakers and consultants—the highest profile and most respected in their fields. One day Jane asked Arlene for a proposal on a special project. When Jane received the proposal, she said, "Arlene, I don't know if I can afford you." Arlene knew this was a smokescreen because of Jane's pattern of buying the best. She quickly reminded Jane of previous discussions about what she was trying to achieve and how her program would accomplish Jane's goals. Jane never said another word about price, and Arlene got the deal.

Caving on price will drag you down. It will cause you to do the following:

- *Lose Your Credibility:* If you cut your price, your new customer will be paying less than your treasured client who made the referral. And you can be certain that your older client company will hear about this discount. Both your credibility and your old good client will be lost forever.
- *Lose Your Reputation:* Word spreads quickly— especially within tightly knit community, cultural, and social groups. People in the same industry talk to each other. You will be known as the company that's an easy mark. With a soft reputation on holding price, you'll be forced to cave in on your negotiations and will rarely be able to get your price again.
- *Lose Your Best Customers:* It's a self-fulfilling

prophecy: If you start taking bad business and working with the wrong customers, you'll become known for working with them, and that will attract more of the same. If you work with your Ideal Customer only, you will gain a superior reputation, and referrals will follow.

• *Lose Your Company:* The future of your company could be threatened. If you continue to play the price game, your margins will be squeezed so tightly that not only will you become unprofitable, but you might have to lay off employees, reduce commissions, and perhaps even close your doors because your service levels have deteriorated beyond recognition.

A PITA customer will erode your profits and perhaps even put you in the red. We would never ask them for a reference or a referral. So why do we take bad business? Because letting go of a customer is a difficult decision in any economy. Companies would rather have some business than no business.

Joanne's Point of View

▼

Fire the PITA customer!

Once you start refusing bad business, you will have gained the opportunity to attract the kind of customers with whom you want to work. One of my clients, Arthur, provides creative services to many large and prestigious companies, and he pushed back vehemently when I said that good customers do not make decisions on price only. Arthur told me that his client companies dictate the price and the terms of engagement. Unless he goes along with this way of doing business, he can't play. He said it was a dilemma, and asked what could he do.

The Ideal Customer

I suggested to Arthur that he had a choice. Yes, he may decide to work with PITAs for a while, because he needs them in his portfolio. However, now that his sales team is shifting to referral selling, they can ask specifically for their Ideal Customer. The balance of the kind of customers they are working with will begin to shift, profits will increase, and these new customers will be terrific referral sources to others just like themselves.

How can you avoid ending up with PITA customers? I believe it's knowing precisely what your Ideal Customer looks like. When you can easily describe and recognize your Ideal Customer, you'll also be less likely to end up with another PITA.

It is our job as salespeople to attract good business. Therefore it is essential for us to be absolutely clear about the kind of clients with whom we want to work. We need to be able to describe our Ideal Customer to ourselves and to everyone we talk to. In my business, I have three criteria for my Ideal Customer:

1. I must have the expertise for the project.
2. The client must value my expertise.
3. The project and the client must be fun.

If clients don't meet these criteria, I refer them to someone else, or I decline the work with a valid excuse.

I actually fired one of my first customers, and it was the best decision I ever made.

There were two partners in an IT business. They wanted to grow their business quickly and were looking for a consultant and a business developer. One of the partners, Joe, had attended my No More Cold Calling workshop. He introduced me to his partner, Dan, and we had many robust discussions. Dan asked me to submit a proposal. Before I submit a proposal, I always ask the client about deadlines and the format he would like it in. We came to an agreement, and I submitted my proposal.

One day later, I received an e-mail from Dan asking me to compile my remarks in a different format, and he mentioned in passing that he would like my comments before noon the next day. I sat there looking at his e-mail, and I grew angrier and angrier. My body tensed, and my face was flushed. I took a deep breath, walked around, and decided within a few minutes to do what I tell my clients to do: Say no.

It was obvious from Dan's request and his continual questions about price that he did not value my expertise. And I was beginning to think that these guys were no fun. Everything was going to be uphill, and I would be drained. I called Dan and Joe and told them that they would be better served working with someone else. The minute I hung up the phone, I felt as if a huge weight had been lifted from my shoulders. I could now move on and find the business that was best for me.

But Wait—Isn't It Just Good Customer Service?

How can you tell if you have a PITA customer or just a customer who is asking for good service? Where does good customer service end and PITA begin? Customers will always try to take advantage of us and to get away with as much as they can. Don't you? What do you do when your computer or other appliance malfunctions, and the company tells you to check its website for information on the fix? No, I don't want to check the website—I paid for the product, and I want to talk to a real person and have him tell me how to fix my problem. And I don't want to pay the company to fix its own problem. However, when I've been referred, I will never take advantage. I have too much respect for the person who referred me and for the company I choose to work with.

Clark, an insurance agent, told me that he has customers who call him constantly with every little question about their policies. These are typically the customers who hold only one policy, and a small one at that. Even after he explains the details of the policy, they will call him again and ask the same questions—seemingly forgetting that they already have an answer. Clark is not in a position to fire these customers because he works for a large company, but he is in a position to avoid these PITA customers in the future. When he asks for referrals, he will ask for exactly the opposite—a customer who is educated, values his time, and is willing to hold several policies with his company.

It's Time!

I've given you my criteria for my Ideal Customer, and now you must develop your own. Consider what you need to have in place to do your best work. For me—and for you—it's not about the number of proposals we write or the number of clients we have. It's about getting those clients who are the opposite of PITA. You want clients who value what you have to offer, communicate well, are forward-thinking, are reasonable, have a good sense of humor, and will give the time, money, and resources to make the project successful. Plenty of these people exist out there. We just need to ask for them. Remember, we get what we ask for!

We need to think like artists when we describe our Ideal Customer. The more definition and color we include, the easier it will be for others to envision people to refer. Think of a recent visit you made to a museum, or look at the artwork in your office. The paintings with the most detail are the ones that are easiest to understand. If you're in a museum, compare a Rembrandt with a Jackson Pollock. Which gives you the clearest picture of the subject matter?

I was working with one of my associates—a salesman for an insurance company. I said that I'd like to refer some clients to him. But first, I needed to ask, "Who is your Ideal Customer?" and "What is a good lead for you?" His answer was, "Anyone who has assets to protect." I told him that was practically the entire universe, and it was way too broad for me to think of anyone. After much conversation he identified two groups that would be an ideal match for his skills and resources: families with young children about to buy a house, and dry cleaners (his company underwrote dry cleaners). That was a lot easier for me to understand than "anyone who has assets to protect."

Salespeople frequently say that they can talk to "anyone who . . ." No. It's not "anyone." "Anyone" all too frequently turns out to be a PITA customer, the one who plays the nickel-and-dime game.

Specificity in asking for what we want is counterintuitive. We often think that if we don't mention everything we do, then we will be leaving something important out, and people won't "get us" completely. This is exactly the opposite of what happens. The more specific you are, the easier it will be for someone to refer you. Listing a bunch of things you do—separated by commas—only confuses people.

My client Linda learned this lesson about expertise when she first started her company. She prepared a brochure about her company and showed it to a former client. The client reviewed it, and Linda never forgot what she said. The client was in a position to make a substantial number of referrals within her company, and she was pleased that Linda had identified a specific niche, because she now knew exactly whom to refer to her. She wanted to feel confident in referring someone with the credentials to do the job and hated it when consultants told her they could do everything. When consultants said they could do everything, she didn't know what category to put them in and wouldn't feel comfortable referring them. What a great lesson for Linda to learn as she started her business!

Now, I want you to pretend that you have a magic wand in your hand while imagining your Ideal Customer. I want you to wave that magic wand as high and as furiously as you can. Seem silly? I actually have magic wands in my workshops, and everyone laughs and waves them. Now you can do the same. How many opportunities do you have to create your Ideal

Customer? You are about to create a profile of your Ideal Customer.

Complete the Ideal Customer Profile worksheet (see p. 98) by thinking about these aspects:

Industry: In what industry do you want to work, or where does your company have a track record?

Geography: Where would you like to work—regions of the United States, North America, Europe, Asia, Middle East, Africa?

Size Company: How large is your ideal company, and how do you measure its size (i.e., number of employees, revenue, age, geographical coverage)?

Business Unit or Function: What group of people within the company are your ideal contacts—CEO, CIO, COO, HR, sales, marketing?

Kind of Person: What are the personality traits (sense of humor, responsible, dedicated, integrity) of your Ideal Customer? Avoid the PITA customer.

Situation or Need: What would a potential client say that would trigger someone to think of referring you? Here are some ideas: "My salespeople aren't performing," "Our teams are not working together," "We've just acquired another company," "We have difficulty recruiting the right talent," "We don't have enough clients," "Our systems are at capacity," "We'll be acquiring more companies," "Morale is low."

As an example, my Ideal Customer is a VP of sales or the head of a sales team who must increase the performance of his sales force and who wants more quality clients. He is willing to spend the time and resources to implement a Referral-Selling System. My Ideal Customer must have an open mind, value my expertise, and be fun to work with. If people want more information after this, I tell them that I work mostly in service businesses in North America. My business partners travel globally to deliver our programs. I will also give them several client examples so that they can clearly picture the results of the work we do.

ACTION STEP 12

Your Ideal Customer

Complete the worksheet (see p. 98) to help you define your Ideal Customer. Keep your magic wand waving!

Now that you've completed this worksheet, take a moment to review your existing client base and your prospects. How closely do they match your ideal?

I was working with one of my clients, Essex Credit, a national lender specializing in boating and recreational vehicle (RV) purchases. Each person completed the worksheet individually, and then we compiled the Ideal from each person's comments. The CEO of the company was in the room and was an active participant in the discussion. Finally we had a clear picture of what the company's Ideal Customers looked

Ideal Customer Profile

▼

Industry	
Geography	
Size of Company	
Business Unit/ Function	
Kind of Person	
Situation/Need	

Important You can choose your customers. You get what you ask for, so ask for what you want! The more specific you are, the easier it will be for someone to refer you.

like: They would be wealthy, have liquidity, be easy to work with, would currently own a boat, and would want to trade up. The CEO looked at the list of qualities, reflected for a moment or two, and then observed that very few of their current customers actually matched this profile: Most were buying smaller boats, and many had credit issues. Essex realized that it took just as long to underwrite a small loan as it did a large loan. It made a decision almost on the spot: Of course it would continue working with customers who wanted to purchase boats of any size. But, when its salespeople were asking for referrals, they would describe their Ideal Customer.

Everyone agreed that if they were able to attract their Ideal Customer consistently, they would be more efficient with each customer, they would need fewer customers, and they would have more referrals, because the boating community is tightly

---

If you want a boat or RV loan, let me take this opportunity to refer you to Essex Credit at 866-377-3948 or www.essexcredit.com.

---

knit, and boat or RV owners will easily relate a good experience to each other. Now, almost a year later, Essex has also discovered that the right customers are more likely to appreciate that they are getting a good deal, and the deals that are coming from referrals close faster and with less hassle. Once again, Essex has realized that a referred customer is a more valuable customer.

And there is a cascade effect: If you work with your Ideal Customers only, you will gain a superior reputation, and more referrals will inevitably follow.

Target Market vs. Ideal Customer

How is being able to describe your Ideal Customer different from focusing on a specific target market? Here's the difference. Target market is a marketing term. Marketing folks do careful analyses on a product's competition, positioning, and messaging, and on their customers' demographics and segmentation. Think about looking for that perfect mate. Marketing people are good at telling you where you are more likely to find him or her (the lobby of a theater), but they are less likely to tell you who they are. Market research offers some meaningful generalities. But your Ideal Customers are specific. It's our job as salespeople to take the information we receive from our marketing departments and enhance it. We need to ask ourselves the following questions when marketing hands us a picture of a target market:

- How is this information helpful to me?
- How does this information apply to my customers?
- How does this information fit with the way I work and the way I communicate value to my customers? Is this my voice?

Market research is the beginning. It provides a great knowledge base, and it is now that our job as expert salespeople begins.

What If Your Organization Doesn't Buy Into Your Ideal Customer Vision?

Can we always attract our Ideal Customers? I believe that we can and we *must*. If you own your own company, you can set the criteria for your organization. You are the one who can say no and support your salespeople in saying no as well. If you work for a large organization, consistently finding your Ideal Customer may be tougher.

You may be handed leads and be expected to follow up on them. Your company may insist that you negotiate (give on price) on some deals. But you can still choose the clients with whom you want to work. There are a couple of things you can do:

- With the discretionary time you have to develop new business, you should absolutely ask for referrals to your Ideal Customer.
- When you're handed leads, you can qualify them based on your Ideal Customer. If there are red flags, you can bring them to the attention of your company and determine whether you want to pursue the prospects.
- You can begin to educate others in your company about the pitfalls of attracting bad business and the successes you've had in attracting profitable referral business.

There are two parts to attracting your Ideal Customer. Part one is asking for what you want. Part two is saying no.

In 1993 I was working with a company that had just completed a major downsizing and reorganization. It had almost gone out of business because it had spread itself too thin. The company had been accepting business that was outside its area of expertise, and it was losing money. To turn things around, it established targets for its business that were in what it called the "strike zone." That was business it could deliver well and on which it made money.

In the first three months I was there, the company turned down two potential opportunities because they were not in the strike zone. Almost miraculously, strike-zone companies began to show up to fill the void, and the company began to be known for its expertise and focus in the exact area in which it wanted to be recognized.

ACTION STEP 13

Research Your Current Customers

- Analyze your current customer base and determine which clients match your Ideal Customer profile.
- Agree as an organization on the criteria for your Ideal Customer.
- Say no if a prospect does not meet your criteria.

There are some traps to avoid as you begin to ask for your Ideal Customer.

- What if you have many capabilities and you feel constrained by my suggestion to be specific?

Most companies have a variety of products and services. Here's what you do. Describe your various areas of expertise to different people. As an example, if you work for an accounting firm, people already know you do taxes and audits. However, you also need to tell potential customers about estate planning, business valuation, insurance services, and merger and acquisition work. How will you decide what to discuss? Find out about their interests first—their clients and their best business. Then choose an example of your capabilities, and describe it.

- What if you are still afraid that if you leave something out by not describing everything you do, you'll miss an opportunity?

Here's where you need to trust me. No company can be all things to all customers. Every organization has, at the very least, an idea of its best customers. Every organization has a best geographical fit. The approach I'm suggesting has been tested and proven time and time again. If what you're doing is working, keep doing it. If it's not, it's time to try something new.

You'll find that people will no longer be confused about the best leads to give you. You will elicit some remarkable suggestions about people you should meet. Your biggest challenge will be following up on all your great leads. You'll be talking to exactly the people you want to meet and who want to meet you, and you will begin to see that you can actually have fewer leads and get more business. You'll be looking for love in all the right places!

CHAPTER 8

Include Everything—
Even the Kitchen Sink

When most people start moving over to referral selling, they don't realize that the best sources of referrals are already all around them. Some people may even think they have tapped out their resources or that they do not know enough people. If you have just joined a new company or moved to a new area, you are probably questioning how you can even start building your referral-selling network.

Here are a couple of illustrations:

- *You've tapped out your resources:* Or have you? I was working with a group of seasoned salespeople—all had sold for more than twenty-five years. As we began to brainstorm to discover people who could possibly be sources of referrals, one of the participants suddenly let out a whoop. He couldn't believe that he'd never even thought of speaking to his neighbor, who he'd known for years. His neighbor worked for a company he wanted to contact. Indeed, he spoke with him and got a perfect referral.

- *You do not know enough people:* You have probably forgotten about all of the people you *do* know. If you've just graduated from college, there are tons of people you know. If you've just returned to the workforce, there are dozens of people you know from all walks of life. I heard a complaint from one of my clients that she was a new mom and had just joined a new company. All of her contacts were other moms. How would *they* know anyone? After our workshop she began talking to these moms and was amazed by the contacts they had. She even went one step further and spoke with their husbands. As a result of these conversations, her network of contacts expanded dramatically.

- *You just joined a new company:* One of my clients, Michele, had just joined a new company. Michele has a big network and had begun contacting folks she knew. After attending No More Cold Calling, she wrote me about the fabulous results she had achieved in just six weeks. She asked for and received eleven referrals, and they all resulted in meetings. All were qualified. Most of the referrals were at the executive level, and a few were at the management level. You might wonder why people would refer you if they don't know what you do. They will refer you because they know and trust you as a person. They know that you have integrity, you do what you say you're going to do, and you'll have the same track record at your new company. Remember, people buy *you* first and *then* what you have to offer. It's about the people you know, not where you work.

• *You just moved into a new area:* Of course you don't know many people. How do you start? You start by identifying professional groups you can join. Join and become active. Don't forget the Realtor who sold you the house or rented you the apartment, the banker, the mortgage broker, your movers (if they are from the area), and then all the people you meet shopping to get set up: at the hardware store and other retailers. Contact people you knew before you moved. With the Internet, wireless, and instant communication, people know everyone everywhere. Distance doesn't matter anymore.

My daughter had survived four layoffs at her company but was a victim of the fifth. She was given ample notice, so she sent an e-mail to everyone on her contact list. One of the people on the list was an acquaintance of hers—now living in North Carolina—from high school in San Francisco. This person wrote back that my daughter had to interview with a certain company in the Bay Area. Her sister-in-law worked for this company, and she was going on maternity leave. My daughter got the interview.

I'm sure you've heard many stories like this before. One of my workshop participants, a financial planner with a large brokerage firm, had just moved from Canada to the San Francisco Bay Area. She wasn't sure that my No More Cold Calling workshop would be effective, since she didn't know anyone here. One of the first things she did was contact her clients in Canada and get referrals to people they knew in the Bay Area. She tapped into numerous other relationships and was amazed at how many of the referrals she received were truly qualified. As a result of the workshop, she was able to leverage her referral network and quickly built a new client base.

So find the people in the place you're leaving who know people where you're going. Or, if you've already arrived, reach back to where you were and see who knows people where you are now. No matter where you are or where you move, your network just continues to expand.

You will now research all of your potential sources of referrals. You'll build your own Referral Wheel, which will include categories of people who could be Referral Sources. Once you complete the Wheel, you will be able to quickly generate names of at least a hundred potential referrals for you to contact.

The key point to remember is that it's not who these people are, it's about the people they know. You don't know who their brother-in-law is, where they used to work, their next-door neighbor, or any of their myriad contacts. And you won't know whom they know until you ask. The average person knows hundreds—even thousands—of people. Some people whom you guess aren't well connected will surprise you. They could be the head of membership for their church, or they could be active in their college alumni association, which has thousands of members. Having one hundred people on your

Referral Wheel can put you one call away from thousands of people or more.

We often assume that certain people won't be good referrals. We run a tape in our heads that says, "Oh, they wouldn't know anyone." So we never ask. I have been surprised time and time again by the people whom others know. We tend to stereotype people and put them into categories. We judge people by their age, the way they dress, the way they speak, the cars they drive, and the people they know. It's called First Impression Management. The good news is that when we're right, it saves time. But when we're wrong, it's a missed opportunity.

I had been working for several months with a public relations firm. One of the people I met was the person in charge of IT. He was a self-proclaimed geek, and what he loved to do the most was to sit in front of his computer creating programs. He called me one day and asked to meet for coffee. He had a project he wanted to sell internally, and he sought my advice.

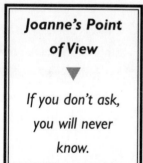

Joanne's Point of View

▼

If you don't ask, you will never know.

We met, and throughout the conversation, I kept telling myself that I should be asking him for referrals. After all, he was familiar with my work and the results I delivered. But I kept saying to myself, "Who would he know?" He was a techie, and he was also very young. I finally asked. To my amazement, he immediately told me of a perfect prospect that was five minutes from my office. I asked him how he knew this company. He said that his aunt had worked there for years, and he had worked there during summer vacations from college. I would never have known unless I had asked.

Your goal is to have a team of people out there selling, promoting, and referring business to you. The Referral Wheel is just the starting point. To get things rolling, you will need to break the habit of ruling out people too quickly. Give it a chance, and soon you'll be hearing compelling stories about the amazing people whom others know.

I know you're going to get so excited about building your Referral Wheel that you'll be tempted to start making calls immediately. Don't! Just get your Wheel built, and then you'll have one more step to complete in the next chapter.

Building Your Referral Wheel

Now is the time to brainstorm categories of people who could possibly be sources of referrals. You know the rules of brainstorming—no judging or evaluating. On each spoke of this Referral Wheel, write a category. Add more spokes if you need them. If you get stumped, check the end of this chapter for some other ideas.

ACTION STEP 14

Build Your Referral Wheel

Complete the Referral Wheel (see p. 111) by listing categories of people who could be potential Referral Sources.

Referral Wheel

Using the Referral Categories and Names worksheets (see pp. 114–5), review your Referral Wheel and identify the referral categories that you think will be most advantageous for you. Write those categories in the spaces provided, and list as many names of people you know in each category. Then in the Priority column, rank the list from 1 to 3. Give a 1 to the people you know best and would feel the most comfortable asking for referrals. Assign 2 to the next group and 3 to the last group. Your final ranking will be organized with the people you know the very best at the top.

ACTION STEP 15

Referral Categories and Names

Complete the Referral Categories and Names worksheet and assign a priority number to each person.

Which category do you think is absolutely the best source of referrals? Current clients? You bet! They already know what you do, how you work, and the results you have achieved. Former clients are equally valuable resources.

Surprisingly, I have found that the least productive category is family. They generally don't understand what we do. I had a situation in my own family. For many years I sold exclusively to the banking industry. Even though I left that focus in 1993, my family on the East Coast continued to ask me if I was still selling to banks. On a recent trip to see my family at an East Coast resort, I gave one of my current audiotapes on No More Cold Calling to my uncle. His daughter, my cousin, arrived unexpectedly and decided to take a run on the beach. She knew her dad always had good music in his headset. So, she grabbed the headset from his room and went for a run. That evening, she looked at me and said, "Now I finally understand what you do." I had no idea what she was talking about until she told me that my audiotape was in her dad's player, and that's what she listened to. Now they get it—over ten years later. Probably not fast enough to provide a basis for building your business.

REFERRAL CATEGORIES

Here are some great categories that are frequently overlooked.

Lost Business

Once in a while you will lose business to a competitor. Clients never like to deliver bad news, and if you have gotten this far in the sales process, you know each other pretty well. The fact that they chose someone else does not mean that you don't have a good offering. Most likely it means one of two things: a senior executive had a stronger relationship with the other company, or the decision-making team felt it could work better with another company.

What do you have to lose by asking this client for a referral? You know your contact is feeling bad—maybe even guilty. I always ask myself the question, "What's the worst that can happen?" If I'm okay with the answer, I go ahead.

Referral Categories and Names

▼

Referral Category	Names	Priority
1	1.	
	2.	
	3.	
	4.	
	5.	
	6.	
	7.	
	8.	
2	1.	
	2.	
	3.	
	4.	
	5.	
	6.	
	7.	
	8.	
3	1.	
	2.	
	3.	
	4.	
	5.	
	6.	
	7.	
	8.	

Referral Categories and Names

▼

Referral Category	Names	Priority
4	1.	
	2.	
	3.	
	4.	
	5.	
	6.	
	7.	
	8.	
5	1.	
	2.	
	3.	
	4.	
	5.	
	6.	
	7.	
	8.	
6	1.	
	2.	
	3.	
	4.	
	5.	
	6.	
	7.	
	8.	

Years ago I had an opportunity for a very large piece of business. My company received an RFP in our San Francisco office. The company sending the RFP didn't know us very well. We conducted many interviews and prepared a beautiful custom proposal. We made the cut and were asked to do a presentation. The proposal was for advanced sales training. I asked my contact why her company wasn't using its current sales training vendor, and she said that the company didn't have an advanced program. Over the course of several months (due to the client's heavy travel schedule), we had more meetings and phone conversations. I was then told we were one of two companies being considered.

Bottom line—they chose the other vendor—the same vendor they were currently using for sales training. In the months that had gone by, the other vendor had developed the program they wanted. My contact felt terrible. She complimented me on my professionalism and wished she could help more. I invited her and other members of her team to lunch. Over lunch, I asked them for referrals to other parts of their organization. She immediately thought of three people and said she would be glad to put me in touch with them.

She then said something I have never forgotten. "Joanne, I am giving these referrals to you, and not to your company." What that meant was that if I had left my company the next day, I could not have handed those referrals to my successor. My client trusted *me*. Making internal referrals was a reflection on her, and she would only refer those she liked and trusted. Wow, what a lesson! This experience also reinforced the fact that unless people like you, they will never do business with you.

Airplane

What kind of conversations do you have on airplanes or while waiting for airplanes?

As I took my seat on a flight to China, the person next to me turned out to be the president of his company and was considering opening business in China. After we spoke for a while, he asked me what I did. I gave him my name and said my company is called No More Cold Calling. "I thought your voice was familiar!" he said. He said he had been on one of my introductory phone calls a month before. We spent a lot of time talking about his business. I had some suggestions for him, and he told me to call him when I returned, and that he'd be glad to help me get business in the Silicon Valley in any way he could. And he has.

On another travel adventure I was waiting for my plane at Chicago's Midway International Airport. Storm clouds were looming, and our flight experienced delay after delay. Those of us in front of the line took seats on the floor and got to know each other. One man, Fred, said that I looked really familiar. It turned out that he lives down the street from me. We quickly asked the standard question: "What brought you to Chicago?" In a matter of minutes, we learned what each other did, and Fred offered to connect me with his marketing manager. All I told him was that my company was called No More Cold Calling, I was the country's leading expert on referral selling, and that I got salespeople in front of the people they wanted to

meet and who wanted to meet them. After a two-minute conversation a neighbor was willing to refer me on the spot.

I soon met with his marketing manager, but it was clear that
we did not have a fit. She said that she met with me because Fred
suggested it. The next words out of her mouth were, "I do know
where you would be a perfect fit." Her previous job was at a
major television station in the Bay Area, and she offered to refer
me to her friend, the director of sales. She told me the politics of
the station, what their issues were, and she made an e-mail introduction. All of this from a chance meeting at an airport.

It's been said that when we travel by plane, the standard "six
degrees of separation" becomes "two degrees of separation."
Why? Because the people you're traveling with are either head-
ing out to the same place you are or are headed home. Either
way, you have a lot in common and could easily know the same
people. When you're delayed, everyone is in the same boat—ag-
itated, annoyed, and tired. So I always smile and say hello to
people and ask them if they're going home or visiting. Most of
the time I talk to really nice people. I pass the time pleasantly,
I learn something, and sometimes I even get a new client!

Kids

Think of all the parents you know through your children
or your friends' children. One of my clients, Tim, took his son
to a soccer game every week. He often sat next to another dad
because their kids were friendly. You know that after a while
the conversation always gets around to what you do for a living. When the other dad asked Tim about his business and
Tim explained, the other dad said that Tim's services were des-

perately needed in his company, and that they should schedule a time to talk. This casual meeting at a child's soccer game resulted in hundreds of thousands of dollars of business.

Exercise

Do you go to the gym? Do you run, hike, or walk? I know you might try to get away from work when you are exercising, but it's also a time to think and reflect. As one of my clients was running with her running partner, she told him about the kind of clients she was looking for and asked him for a referral. He knew exactly the person she needed to meet, and he facilitated the introduction.

Service Providers

One of my clients, Jennifer, had taken her car into her mechanic for a minor repair. While she was waiting, she got into a conversation with the owner of the repair shop. She asked him if he knew any companies that needed worker's compensation or property and casualty insurance. This kind of insurance is fairly specialized. It's not something every one needs every day. Jennifer had almost ruled out the mechanic as a potential refer-

---

If you need property and casualty or worker's compensation insurance and want to work with a company that is well informed and will pay attention to you, contact Alliant Resources Group at www.alliantresourcesgroup.com. How do I know Alliant Resources Group? Its VP of human resources was one of my first clients. (She was referred, of course.) She joined Alliant in the same capacity and hired me to speak at an incentive trip for its top producers.

ral source, but she decided to ask anyway. The mechanic referred her to one of his customers, and Jennifer got a new client.

Another client, Max, related a story that I have never forgotten. Max was downsized from his company. As an executive he was able to take advantage of outplacement counseling. One of his assignments was to ask ten people a week for a referral to a prospective employer. During a holiday celebration his sink backed up, and he had to call a plumber. Max knew that he was running behind on his promise to ask ten people, so he decided to ask the plumber. Much to Max's surprise, the plumber was going to the house of a CEO the next day. The plumber told the CEO about Max. Max got the interview, and Max got the job. This may sound unbelievable, but like the other stories in this book, it's true.

Now that you've heard these stories, you've probably thought of many other people you could ask for referrals.

ACTION STEP 16

Creating Your List of One Hundred

- Using your database, go through your address book and think of people you've met on trips, schoolmates, neighbors, and even people from your previous job. One person will make you think of the next . . . and the next . . . and the next.
- Prioritize the list with those you know the best at the top.
- Share the list with your Business Buddy.

Remember, it's not about who these people are, it's about the people they know. And you don't know the people they know until you ask. You have begun to bring referral selling to life. Now you have a plan, but please don't start asking for referrals yet! In the next chapters you'll learn to be so compelling in your message that no one could possibly resist you. You'll learn a step-by-step process to ask for referrals so that you'll get in front of the people you want to meet and who want to meet you—every time. This is what referral selling is about!

The Referral Wheel Memory Joggers

▼

Over the past years No More Cold Calling workshop participants have brainstormed all the possible referral sources they encounter. This index is meant to jog your memory and help you create your potential referral list. Those shown in bold are the ones we feel are the best Referral Sources.

- ❑ Airplane & other strangers
- ❑ Alumni groups
- ❑ Associations
- ❑ Boards of directors
- ❑ Brokers
- ❑ Business groups
- ❑ Chambers of commerce
- ❑ Children—groups, events
- ❑ Civic groups
- ❑ Coffee shops
- ❑ Colleagues/peers
- ❑ Community/ volunteer groups
- ❑ Competitors
- ❑ Complementary fields
- ❑ Consultants
- ❑ **Current clients**
- ❑ Educational institutions/ schools

- ❑ Employees
- ❑ Family
- ❑ **Former clients**
- ❑ Former coworkers
- ❑ Friends
- ❑ Health clubs
- ❑ Industry associates
- ❑ Influencers
- ❑ Investors
- ❑ Kids
- ❑ **Lost business**
- ❑ Neighbors
- ❑ Networking groups
- ❑ Noncompeting businesses
- ❑ Patron of businesses (mechanic, dry cleaner)
- ❑ Personal services (hairstylist, massage)
- ❑ Political organizations
- ❑ Professionals (CPA, attorney, banker)

- ❑ Prospects you turned down
- ❑ Recreational groups
- ❑ Recruiters
- ❑ Religious organizations
- ❑ Salespeople in other businesses
- ❑ Social engagements
- ❑ Spouses
- ❑ Strategic alliances
- ❑ Students
- ❑ Tenants in buildings where you work/live
- ❑ Trade associations
- ❑ Travel/commuting
- ❑ Vendors
- ❑ Volunteer groups
- ❑ Web networking
- ❑ Weddings
- ❑ Workshop partners

CHAPTER 9

Looking Good:
The Secret of Attraction

If asking for referrals were easy, most companies would have more than enough business. In chapter 2 we reviewed some of the reasons referral selling is not the passion of every salesperson, every sales manager, and every executive: Most people are just plain uncomfortable asking for referrals. The fact is, referral selling is a skill—we need to know *how* to ask.

The good news is that there's a proven way to ask for referrals—a system that will provide you with a comfortable and effective way to get in front of the customers you want to meet and who want to meet you. You will learn a process to consistently attract your Ideal Customers. As you refine the process, you will become better and better at asking for referrals. You will realize that you have already earned the right to ask for referrals from anyone you want—and from more people than you ever imagined.

atTRACT New Customers

The process is called atTRACT, because referrals are the best way to attract more clients. There are five steps: Tell, Remind, Audience, Contacts, and Touch base. I will introduce each step in the process and demonstrate how I use it. As you practice and use the steps, you will need to adapt the process to your own personality and style.

Your Referral Source

You will be using atTRACT when you are talking with anyone that you've identified on your Referral Wheel in the previous chapter. Anyone whom you want to refer you is a Referral Source.

One of my clients is very quick-witted and uses a lot of humor with her clients. She told me that the more she practiced asking for referrals, the more comfortable she was making the language and style her own. The words just flowed. One time, as she was describing her Ideal Customer, she suddenly paused, smiled, and then said, "Someone just like you." The customer broke up laughing. He gave her a referral immediately, and before she returned to the office, the referral had called. She was able to close a deal similar in dollar value as her Referral Source. She was beginning to make herself attractive!

Here are the five steps in the process of asking for referrals. It is critical to follow each step.

Tell

I begin the conversation with my Referral Source by explaining that I build my business through referrals. It is a statement of fact. Stating that you build your business through referrals is a powerful positive statement you are making about yourself. You are also stating, without having to put it into words, that you are confident about who you are and what you are selling, and that you are willing to stand on your reputation.

There are three reasons we need to Tell:

1. **Our clients don't spend their days worrying about how to grow our businesses:** We often mistakenly assume that our clients, friends, and business associates know we want more clients and that we would like them to refer us. But they are focused on their own businesses, their challenges, and their families. Even I, the Referral Queen, am frequently asked how I get new business. People who have just met me usually don't believe that I could build a successful company solely on referrals.

2. **Good work is not enough:** We assume that if we've delivered results for our clients that they will refer us. Maybe, maybe not. Our clients are focused on the day-to-day workings of their businesses. It is not top of mind for them to refer clients to us. They may even believe that if they refer us, we will have less time to dedicate to their projects.

3. **We might appear to be too busy already:** Some people assume that appearing to be incredibly busy with client work will send the message that they're successful, and that will translate into more business. The

fact is, if it appears that we're overwhelmed, who would feel as if they're going to get our best work? I have one client who always talks about the hours she works—in the office at 6 A.M. and on many Sundays. Who would ever think that she would want or need more clients? But she does. She is a partner in a prestigious, privately held accounting firm, and she has recently opened a new office and is expected to build business in this new area. She might have said, "I'm busy with some great projects, but I'm always looking for a few terrific new clients."

REMIND

Before we can ask for referrals, we need to remind our contacts of the value or results that we deliver.

If your Referral Source is a current client, you should lead a discussion about the results that they have already achieved by working with you. Remind them of why they made the decision to work with you, and find out specifics about how your solution has impacted their business results.

You may think that reminding clients of your accomplishments is reminding them of the obvious, but they have gone on to run their businesses and their lives. The work you did has long since been absorbed into everything else. They are probably so satisfied with you that they take you for granted. You need to remind them of life before your solution was implemented.

You can open the process by asking a few leading questions:

- How does your client feel about the service you have delivered? What has the client's experience been working with you?
- Why did your client choose you over your competition, and has their judgment been validated?
- What results have been achieved—what savings in dollars have been realized, what improved processes are now in place, or what problems have gone away?

Dig deep and ask what you can do going forward to make the relationship even more valuable. Ask the client to discuss the business results from your project, the benefits their company received, and why it was so great to work with you. Quantify your results as much as possible. There is a difference between stating that you "improved the morale of a company's employees," and stating that you "decreased turnover by 10 percent, with a savings of $5 million."

If your Referral Source is not a current client, you will need to have ready several results, or "proof" statements, that reflect the value you typically deliver.

I will give you my example first, because my clients always press me to give examples of what I typically say. Since I have developed and used a Referral-Selling System for years, they want to hear from the expert. My example should trigger some immediate ideas for you and bring home the key points. Your task will then be to create your own results and examples.

- **Reduce Prospecting Time:** No More Cold Calling gets salespeople in front of the people they want to meet and who want to meet them. Our clients skip over those awkward first steps of any sales process—"What am I going to say to begin the conversation?" or "How can I connect with this person?" or "What if the prospect doesn't see the benefit of what I offer?" When we're referred, we engage in a robust business conversation, and the sales process accelerates quickly. Salespeople are now doing what they love to do—meeting with clients—and not hanging on the phone trying to make appointments with people who could care less about what they are offering.

• **Increase Quality Prospects:** Our clients increase their qualified-lead pipeline an average of 30 percent. It's about quality, not quantity. Think about how productive it is to have only viable business in your pipeline.

• **Increase Revenue and Profits:** Our clients increase their referral business by a minimum of 20 percent. Referral customers buy more and have more loyalty over the long term. They are less likely to quibble about price, so we see marked increases in both revenue and profit margins.

• **Get Clients Faster:** The conversion rate of referral prospects to actual clients is typically about 75 percent. This means that for every four potential customers a salesperson meets, three of them will become regular clients. Think about the impact of this kind of selling on your business.

• **Eliminate Unproductive Selling:** Our clients spend less time prospecting and get more business. This is the best part. They spend their time on viable business opportunities, not chasing after business that has a slim chance of closing. Because they are speaking to prospects who are qualified—they have a need and they want to talk—they close more business in less time and spend less time getting to the right people. They've also saved the potential client time in locating the best resource. It's a win-win for everybody.

AUDIENCE

In chapter 7 you identified your Ideal Customer. This is the person you want to meet, or your audience. You will now describe your audience to your Referral Source.

You must be precise in describing your audience, because you're not looking for just anyone. You want a specific kind of person or organization with explicit needs. Your Ideal Customer is the one you want to meet, because this is someone who recognizes the value of your offering, who needs what you have, and is willing and capable of paying for it.

One way to be specific is to ask for a meeting with an executive, such as a CEO or a VP of sales, IT, manufacturing, or HR. Or, it could be more direct, such as targeting a company by name and asking to be connected to certain people in that company.

If you limit your leads to people and organizations that fit the portrait of your Ideal Customer, your conversion rate from lead to customer will soar. Remember, the more specific you are, the easier it will be for others to think of someone to refer.

CONTACTS

You've described your results and clearly profiled who you are looking for. You've now set the stage for your Referral

Source to help. She is fresh in her thinking about you, is current on your business and the value you bring, and clearly sees your vision of your desired audience.

You will now ask your Referral Source for three things:

1. **Who are one or two people you know who match the description of my audience?** Ask for only one or two people because:

   • The first people she thinks of will be the best and the most qualified.
   • It doesn't feel intrusive to ask for only one or two.
   • You will feel comfortable going back to this person and asking for more.
   • One or two is manageable—there is time to follow up.

2. **What did I say that made you think of people to refer?** Once your Referral Source has named one or two people, you need to find out about them. Test and see whether they really match your picture of your Ideal Customer. You need to know enough about their companies and their needs to be able to talk with them intelligently. Ask your Referral Source to tell you as much as she can about the people being referred—their business issues, their competition, and their growth strategies. You need to know enough about the personalities of your audience to know how to read them (no PITA customers). Are

they slow and methodical? Are they numbers-driven? Do they have a strong need to get comfortable over a dinner or a game of golf before business can be discussed? What is the relationship between your Referral Source and the person she is referring?

3. **Contact them now:** This is the single most important step in the atTRACT process. You are asking for *immediate action*. You will now ask your Referral Source to contact your Ideal Customer and introduce you now—while she is still clear on the value and benefits you bring.

Aha! This is where most people become skittish. Yet this step is the key to the success of the entire Referral-Selling System. If you do not ask for the introduction, the atTRACT process will not work. Although this book is money well spent, the time it took you to read it and to do the exercises will have been wasted. If you call someone who doesn't know you and is not expecting your call, or if you call without an introduction, it is a *cold call.*

Wow. Will you actually be able to ask for an introduction? Yes, and by learning to do it, you will revolutionize your life.

Look at this important "before and after" moment in your life. Here is the way you are now: Typically, your Referral Source will say something like, "Just give him a call and tell him I told you to call. He's a great buddy, and I'm sure he will talk to you." Wrong! Without realizing it, your Referral Source is asking you to cold call. Think of the difference between calling and using someone's name versus calling after you have been introduced. Don't delude yourself. If someone is not expecting your call, it is a cold call. Arctic. Iceberg. Freezing. Out in the cold. Your hands are blue and your nose is running. Get the picture? You only want to make *hot* calls. There is no point in making any other kind.

Here is the way you're going to live your sales life in the future: You are respecting your Referral Source's relationship with your Ideal Customer. If your Referral Source is a client, you are offering a solution that has worked for your Referral Source and her company. Of course your Referral Source will want to contact your Ideal Customer and make sure this person understands the importance of the referral. When you and your new customer get together, your relationship will be warm or maybe hot. Maybe even smoking!

There are three, and only three, ways that are acceptable for your Referral Source to introduce you: by phone, by e-mail, or in person. Most people will offer to call their referrals immediately. Some Referral Sources will prefer sending an e-mail. Occasionally, your Referral Source will arrange a personal meeting with the three of you. Any of these is fine.

Phone: Ask your Referral Source to call the contact. Many times she will pick up the phone and call while you are still in the office. Your Referral Source may also offer to make the call in the next few days. That's fine, too.

E-mail: Some people prefer an e-mail introduction. I used to resist e-mail introductions, as my preferred communication style is to call and speak with someone. However, I have seen that in my clients' businesses, and in my own business, too, e-mail introductions have produced significant results. If people want to send e-mails, you should provide them with the text. It should be short, bulleted, and it should address the needs of the person to whom you're being referred.

One of my clients, Scott at Mandel Communications (www.mandelcom.com), crafted an e-mail for his Referral Source. The message not only demonstrated the results Mandel Communications had delivered, but reflected the tone and personality of his Referral Source:

> I'm always looking for ways to give my guys the "juice" or extra edge they need to sell better and higher. I've developed a good relationship with Mandel Communications. We have used them for presentation skills training, combined with specific sales training. The training I asked them to design helped my team connect with our customers at the CXO level. They do a good job and have customer satisfaction scores on their classes that average 9.27 on a 10 scale.
>
> I gave Scott, our Mandel account executive, your names. You might like to talk with him to explore what his firm can do for you.
>
> Cheers

In person: If your Referral Source has a very close relationship with the person she is referring, she may suggest a personal meeting to introduce you to a relative or a lifelong friend. You could get together for coffee, drinks, or a meal.

Here's a story from one of my clients that shows why you need to get in the habit of asking for that referral call immediately.

Steve, from The Marlin Company (The Workplace Communication Experts, www.TheMarlinCompany.com), sold a license deal to a large client two years ago. It was now time for the renewal. The prospect praised the service enthusiastically and signed up for another two years, mentioning in passing other locations under a subordinate manager. Steve picked up on the comment and asked to be introduced to the subordinate. The subscriber got her on the phone and repeated his praise for Steve's service. He did this for five minutes. When he finished, the subordinate said, "If this service is working so well for you, why don't you just sign me up for it, too?" Steve left a few minutes later with a signed order for six more license deals, in addition to the order for the two he'd renewed. Not bad for asking for an introduced referral.

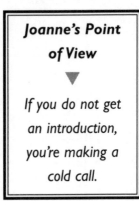

Joanne's Point of View

▼

If you do not get an introduction, you're making a cold call.

"The only thing that bothers me," Steve said, "is that I didn't have a tape recorder running. The subscriber had such great things to say about us and said them so well that I would have liked to replay them from time to time for inspiration."

TOUCH BASE

Keeping in touch with your Referral Source over time will become a source of great pleasure. This is going to be a cherished relationship, so nurturing it begins when your Referral Source gives you your first referral.

Always, always thank your Referral Source for making the referral. You cannot say thank you enough. At a minimum leave a voicemail or send an e-mail. I send a personal note. Most people get so few handwritten notes today that when someone takes the time to do it, people love it. Personal notes are always the mail that gets opened first.

If your company doesn't have note cards, get some of your own. Have your name imprinted, and always have cards handy. Keep a few with you (and some stamps), and write a note when you have a few minutes between appointments. Being timely is important, too. Sending a note two weeks after the event puts you back on ice with your source. Don't let that happen.

> *I have received phone calls thanking me for my thank-you note and asking me where I get my stationery. It comes from Barbara Patinkin at www.classiccommunication.com. She's the greatest!*

Look what happens when you forget to say thank you. I referred an individual to a client of mine who I knew would be a perfect fit. Too many months later I heard from my client that she was doing business with the person I referred. I was delighted that my client had found a good resource, but I was really annoyed that I never heard from the person I referred. Do you think I will rush to refer this person again? Less likely than before.

If your sales cycle is lengthy, keep your Referral Source abreast of your progress with short notes or calls. Always tell this person whether you've won or lost the business, or if the decision has been delayed.

That's it! The five simple atTRACT steps that will end cold calling in your life forever are **T**ell your Referral Sources what you want, **R**emind them of the value you provided, describe your Ideal Customer—your desired **A**udience, ask your Referral Sources for their **C**ontacts and ask them to make the call, and nurture your Referral Sources when you consistently **T**ouch base.

You're done! That's it! Close the book!

Not so fast. I've taught my method long enough to realize that not everyone dashes out and immediately switches to referral selling. There are fears and hesitation about this new, unexplored territory. Let's take a moment to address these fears.

What's Stopping You?

IT FEELS REALLY UNCOMFORTABLE

Asking for the introduction is when most people feel uncomfortable. It doesn't matter whether you are a woman or a man, young or old—the story is the same. You may feel as if you are jeopardizing a relationship—you have a friendship, and bringing in business might shift or even end the friendship. There are many reasons you might feel this way:

- You could be intruding and jeopardizing a trusted relationship.
- You're asking a busy person to do even more work.
- You're afraid of being perceived as asking for help—

it's not really cool in our society to ask for help. It can be considered a sign of weakness.

- If you have to ask for referrals, it must mean your business isn't doing so well.
- It feels pushy and "salesy."
- It feels like begging, or asking for a favor. And then you might owe the person something back.
- The person might say no.

So many excuses. Let's deal with them right now and get rid of them. They are all that stand between you and the beginning of a wonderful new way of creating business relationships.

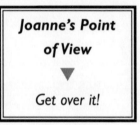

Joanne's Point of View

▼

Get over it!

Think of someone you know and trust—perhaps someone in business or in your personal life. This person came to you and asked you for a referral. It might have been to one of your business contacts or to your banker, mechanic, or insurance agent. You get the idea. Did you make the referral? Of course you did. You give referrals all the time when you are asked—and sometimes even when you are not.

Now I want you to put the shoe on the other foot. If you readily give referrals, why wouldn't others be delighted to do the same for you? Think about that for a minute.

Notice that I said someone came to you whom you *knew* and *trusted*. You have to earn the right to ask. How many times have you been to a business event, met people briefly, and then received lengthy e-mails the next day asking you to refer them? No way. You do not know them and don't know the quality of their work.

I Haven't Earned the Right to Ask

If it's a current client and you've done good work, you have definitely earned the right. They know you, trust you, and will be eager to make a referral—if they're asked.

A well-regarded outplacement firm, I'll call it AllStar Associates, decided to do a customer-satisfaction survey with fifty of its best clients. Among the questions AllStar asked was, "Would you be willing to make a referral to AllStar?" The survey had a 7-point scale, with 7 being the highest in satisfaction. The average answer to this question was 6.5. Fifty of AllStar's best clients said that they would be willing to give a referral. Amazingly, no one at AllStar had ever asked any client for a referral. With the survey in hand, AllStar now realized the enormous untapped potential for new business that was just sitting there. AllStar immediately put a plan in place to shift its business to referral selling.

When you meet someone briefly at a business event, you haven't yet earned the right to ask for a referral. If you've made a connection, schedule another meeting to learn about each other and see if there are ways you could work together. Always consider how you can help someone else first. Asking the question, "How can I help *you*?" is one of the most powerful questions you can ask. (But only ask if you mean it.) Most people are surprised—even startled—when I ask how I can help them. They never expect the question. Some have an immediate response, and others need to think about it. Bottom line: They know I am willing to help them as much as they are willing to help me.

You reconnect with people you haven't seen in years. Why

would they refer you? They will refer you because they know you and trust you. People don't change. People with integrity continue to enhance their credibility.

I was at a fiftieth birthday party for a business colleague and friend. A woman I hadn't seen in years walked in the door. We not only went to the same college, we were in the same sorority. The last time we had seen each other was at least seven years before then. We spent the rest of the evening catching up (much to the chagrin of our husbands). She now sells long-term care insurance and immediately offered to refer me to the president of her company. We had two meetings, and within only two months, her firm became a client.

On another occasion, my husband and I went to a dinner party to honor an old friend of his who was getting married the next day. The evening was a time to reconnect and celebrate this wonderful occasion. I brought the hostess and our friend a gift—samples of an anti-aging skin care product that I have been using for years and now represent. (The results have been so remarkable that when I'm with my daughters, people often ask if we are sisters!) I heard our friend say to her fiancé, "Joanne doesn't do anything that isn't top-notch, so I really want to use these products." (If you want to know how Mother Nature can turn back the hands of Father Time, go to www.joanne black.myarbonne.com.) It doesn't matter what you are selling—if the person knows you, likes you, and trusts you, you have earned the right to ask for referrals.

If you're still uncomfortable about

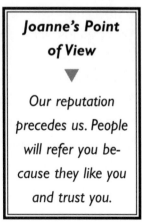

Joanne's Point of View

▼

Our reputation precedes us. People will refer you because they like you and trust you.

asking someone to introduce you, think about it this way: If you wanted to refer someone you knew to a contact of yours, you would always prefer to make the introduction. After all, it is your relationship, and your credibility is on the line.

You need to understand that your Referral Source is doing her contact a favor by referring you. You're asking your Referral Source to be helpful to someone else because your Referral Source knows that you have a solution that will benefit other businesses.

When you are referred, your prospective client has the opportunity to do the following:

- Save tons of time, because your Referral Source has separated you from the crowd. What a relief!
- Be presented with a proven solution and a trusted resource. The prospective client knows they will spend time wisely by meeting with you.

One of my clients, Al, called on the executive director of the assisted living branch of a nursing home chain. It was an introduced referral from one of the subordinate administrators who liked Al's service but couldn't close the deal. Al had asked the subordinate to phone or e-mail the executive director. An e-mail went out, and the executive director received and remembered it. "I've been expecting your call," she told Al, and set the appointment. She bought his service. "I didn't even have to ask her for the order," Al said. "On the contrary," she told me, "I'm glad they sent you my way. This is just what we need." While he was at it, he set an appointment with her to make a presentation to the administrators of her other seven facilities. Anyone want to place a bet on his chances of closing more business?

As you can see, asking for referrals is very, very personal— it's a reflection of the core of who we are. Our biggest fear is that we will be rejected—someone will say no and they won't refer us. We feel vulnerable, and so when we first start on this new path, we may hesitate to ask. But what you will quickly discover is that people won't say no if they're asked the right way—a way that is respectful, clear, and helps them contribute value to others. It's called atTRACT.

I'M ASKING FOR HELP

Yes, you are. We have been taught that adults can appear weak by asking for help. When people contemplate asking for a referral, they frequently get nervous and uncomfortable. The truth is, you are asking for the opportunity to help someone who will benefit from your products and services. If someone helped you find a terrific deal on a car, you'd be delighted to tell others. If someone brought your company a new machine that saved you time and money, you'd be delighted to let others know about it. If you found a bank or a real estate agent or an attorney who had done wonderful work for you, you'd be delighted to let others who needed that service know about it.

People will do exactly the same for you, because human beings like to and want to help each other. Putting good people together just plain feels good. Think what the world would be like if people focused more on helping each other.

Even if people can't help you at that moment, at a minimum you will have raised their awareness for good potential referrals for you. Your Referral Source will be thinking of you and will let you know when she has identified an opportunity. Your goal is to talk to as many Referral Sources as you can. You will be converting these people into your own private sales force that will be taking your message to the world. Soon you will be getting calls from people who want to talk to you. Your biggest challenge at that point will not be lead generation.

ACTION STEP 17

Identify a Practice Partner

- Identify someone you know really well and with whom you can get together, in person, in the next week.
- Schedule a time to meet to practice asking for referrals.

Practice

Initially, I would like you to have the atTRACT conversation in person with someone you know really well—a friend or a peer. Be clear about the purpose of the conversation with your friend. You are sharing a new way to grow your business. It's a strategy that might help your friend as well. Take the time to have a meaningful exchange of ideas and to look for ways to be of assistance to each other.

My mother used to say that practice makes perfect. One of my clients says that practice makes permanent. You will be very tempted to skip the practice—especially if you are a seasoned salesperson. Don't. You need to practice three times *in person* with people you know really well. Remember your list of one hundred? Start with the top three. You're not asking these people for their business, you're asking them for people they know. This is an important distinction and will shift the dynamics of your conversation. Yes, you are asking for their help. They know you and trust you, so why wouldn't they help you? You would do the same for them, and you probably already have.

Remember that it's not about the number of leads you get, but the number of leads you get that are qualified. Activity is important, but mindless activity that focuses only on quantity is bad business. Getting results is about doing less and getting more. Referral selling is about using your past successes and your well-nurtured relationships to build your business. It's like having your own private sales force putting you in touch with people you want to meet and who want to meet with you. Referral selling is about leveraging your successes instead of endlessly starting over by prospecting for cold leads. Your prospecting will never be the same again.

CHAPTER 10

Take It Out for a Spin

Your sole purpose now is to practice asking for referrals and receiving feedback. However, as has been true for many of my clients, you might get referred on your first attempt.

You've identified the person you're going to ask for referrals (your Referral Source) and have scheduled a meeting. If you still have any of those uncomfortable feelings about asking for referrals, now is the time to dispel them. Remember, this person is someone you know really well and who likes and trusts you. You don't need to worry that this person might say no, or that you're intruding on the relationship, or that it feels pushy and "salesy." You have nothing to lose. You could even say, "I just read this terrific book and would like to practice my new business strategy with you."

It's Time!

There are three steps to taking action on your goals: thinking about them, writing about them, and speaking about them.

Our goals are simply not real unless we are willing to proclaim what they are in public.

As for myself, I considered writing this book for more than a year. I took several classes on book writing. I researched proposal writing, spoke to authors, and compared self-publishing versus trying to get an agent and hoping to attract a major publisher. As part of my New Year's resolution for 2003, I announced to my family, friends, and business associates that I was going to write my book. Without realizing it, I had established my own accountability network. I soon began to receive phone calls and e-mails asking, "How's the book coming along?" I was on the hook. Six months later, I began writing my proposal.

Start Writing

We've reviewed the atTRACT process, and you've thought about the person you're going to practice with and what you're going to say. The next step is to write exactly—word-for-word—what you're going to say. Yes, it's a script that may seem artificial, but it's an essential step in your success. When you actually speak it, your message will be in your own voice, and you'll be fine. I promise.

ACTION STEP 18

Write Your Script

Complete the atTRACT worksheet (see p. 148) for the person you are going to meet. Write your contact's name at the top.

Start Asking

You are now ready to meet with a friend or a peer. You know this person well, so you'll probably begin with a conversation about your business and personal lives. Relax. This person is always going to ask you, "What's new?" or "What have you been up to?" This is a perfect time to tell the person you are building your business through referrals and to delve into the atTRACT process. Be sure to include each step in the process.

1. **Tell** your friend that you have a new strategy for building your business. It's called referral selling, and the best way to get a referral is to ask a friend.
2. **Remind:** Set the stage—recite past successes or tell an interesting story.
3. **Audience:** Describe your Ideal Customer.
4. Ask for one or two **Contacts**, and remember to ask for an introduction.

There are three different ways to have the atTRACT conversation.

atTRACT New Business

▼

Contact's name _____

Step 1	**Tell**
Step 2	**Remind**
Step 3	**Audience**
Step 4	**Contacts**
	Ask for contacts _____
	Ask about contact _____
	Ask for introduction _____
Step 5	**Touch Base**
	✉ ❑ Thank-you note sent
	☎ ❑ Follow-up phone call

1. Follow the steps in order.
2. Insert the steps throughout your conversation.
3. Begin with the "Remind" step of atTRACT. A great attention grabber is telling a story about the results your clients have achieved.

Here is an easy way to structure your story:

Situation: What was the situation or problem the client was facing?
Action: What did you do to resolve the problem?
Result: What result did the client achieve by working with you?

As an example, Jessica, my colleague and favorite mortgage broker, tells this story:

Situation: There was a client whose credit score was below the level that would allow him to borrow at the prime rate. He believed that he was two years away from buying his home.

Action: Jessica referred her client to her credit repair partner, and the client's credit score was increased by one hundred points within eight weeks.

Result: Four weeks later the client bought the condo of his dreams in San Francisco.

If you live in the San Francisco Bay Area, are making your next move, buying a vacation home, or buying a rental property, I would like to refer you to Jessica Lanning, Certified Mortgage Consultant, and her team at Triton Funding Group (jlanning@tritonfunding.com or www.jessicalanning.com).

Another way to enhance your story is to include a testimonial. One of my clients, Keith at The Marlin Company, did just that. After attending the No More Cold Calling workshop, Keith called three friends to request referrals. One of them worked for a major manufacturer, and he got Keith an initial appointment that eventually led to a meeting with the VP of HR. The VP was an arch skeptic who looked askance at everything Keith showed her. Finally, Keith said, "I'm not making this up. If you don't believe me, talk to my client yourself." The client raved about the product and the service, and Keith easily wrote the order: a fine sale from an introduced referral and an effective testimonial.

Keep Plugging Away

What If They Can't Think of Anyone?

Your Referral Sources may not be able to think of anyone on the spot. One of three things could be going on:

- They truly can't think of anyone right then.
- They're not absolutely clear about what you need.
- They don't want to say no and will tell you they'll think about it.

The last reason is rare. I've found that about 5 percent of people have no interest in helping. You'll want to focus on the other 95 percent of the people out there. If they can't think of referrals immediately, offer to call them the next week. Follow up with e-mails to remind them of your conversations. Most people are visual learners, and it may jog people's memories if they see something in print. Your e-mail should be crafted so that it describes the work you do and can easily stand alone and be forwarded by your Referral Source. The e-mail is meant to serve two purposes:

1. Looking at what is written rather than what is being spoken can spark additional thoughts.
2. Your Referral Source can easily forward the e-mail to people he knows.

Most important, however, is to ensure that you have described clearly and accurately what you are looking for. I always ask my Referral Source if I was clear enough. He will then typically repeat my Ideal Customer, and I can look for knowledge gaps. If you need a contact in a specific company, name the company. Encourage the Referral Source to think of others in the Referral Wheel. Suggest he think of neighbors, friends, and people in professional organizations. Reflect on any category you think is a fit. You need to expand his thinking, just as you've expanded yours.

You have gained ground, even if you don't receive a referral immediately. At a minimum the person now understands what you do and will think of opportunities for you in the future. I continue to receive referrals from Shelli, whom I worked with over ten years ago. In the last five years she has given me three qualified referrals. Each became a client immediately. Shelli knows what I am looking for, and her referrals are always spot on.

I received an e-mail from someone who was referred by Rod, a person I worked with over fifteen years ago. Rod and I have kept in touch, but I hadn't spoken to him in at least a year. He remembered. That's all that counts.

I offered a public workshop on the East Coast, and a woman who was planning to attend cancelled at the last minute. I only spoke with her once before the workshop, but she continued to receive my follow-up e-mails. I never met her in person. One day I received an e-mail referring me to her professional association as a speaker at their national conference. Eight months later I was called by the conference director asking me to speak. She said that I had come very highly recommended, and she mentioned this fact several times during our conversation. I got the engagement.

You are in the process of building momentum. The more people who know what you do and know that you are building your business through referrals, the more referrals you will receive.

What If They Can't Use Your Service?

You may meet with a prospect, and it's not the right fit, or the prospect doesn't have the budget for it at this time. You can still maximize your sales call. Here's what Mark at The Marlin Company did.

Mark made a presentation to a prospect who wasn't able to buy right then. Following the rule that you should get something out of every call, Mark obtained a referral from the prospect to his friend, who was the president of a small chain of health care facilities. "Let's send him an e-mail right now while you're in front of your computer," Mark suggested. "Sure, why not?" the prospect replied. Mark soon wrote the first of what he hopes will be several sales with the referred prospect. "Thank you, Joanne Black," he adds. "This is my third sale from an introduced referral in the last three months."

Asking with Confidence

Here are some suggestions for asking with confidence. Choose the one you feel most comfortable with, and stick with it for a while:

- It would mean the world to me if you could introduce me to one or two people you know.
- It would be terrific if you could put me in touch with one or two people you know.
- I'd really appreciate it if you could introduce me to one or two movers and shakers.
- It's your relationship, and I know you'll want to make the call to introduce me.
- It really works best if the person making the referral makes the introduction.
- An introduction from you would be terrific. If I just get a name, it's like a cold call (and you know I don't make cold calls).

Traps to Avoid

BEGGING AND PLEADING COMMENTS

Beware of diluting your conversation with begging and pleading comments. These are statements you make because you are not yet comfortable coming right out and asking for a referral. Some are questions that can be answered with no. Others are just not accurate. You might as well hold out a tin cup.

- Do you know anyone . . . (*No*)
- I was wondering . . . (*Are you?*)
- Would you mind . . . (*Really?*)
- Is it possible . . . (*Come on*)
- Would it be OK if . . . (*Of course it will.*)
- Do you have any you'd like to share . . . (*Yuck*)
- I was hoping . . . (*Were you?*)
- Are there one or two people you could refer me to . . . (*No*)

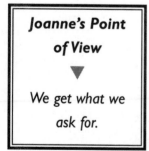

Joanne's Point of View

▼

We get what we ask for.

You've done a great job describing your Ideal Customer. Ask for what you want. No more begging and pleading comments.

SKIPPING STEPS IN THE PROCESS

Mark told me that he loves the at-TRACT process, but his early success led him to get lazy, and he went off course for a while. He stopped telling people that he was building his business through referrals. He didn't clearly describe his Ideal Customer. He left out asking his customers to call or e-mail the prospects while he was still in his Referral Source's office, so when the source got busy, he forgot. Before long Mark wasn't getting referrals.

Mark has since become more disciplined and has had great success with referrals. In his first six months he's asked for and received forty introduced referrals. He has closed fifteen of those, and most of the rest are moving along the sales process. These new customers account for 14 percent of his entire year's business. And the remaining twenty-five referrals will be coming his way shortly.

FORGETTING TO PRACTICE

Now that you've learned the atTRACT process, you might think you're ready to go. Not so fast. Have you ever launched a new product or campaign without piloting it? I doubt it. You need to practice. Practice will ensure that you are conversational, that you include all of the steps, and that you get feedback on what works and what you need to do differently. You're going to practice and have a great time doing it!

One of my clients had been selling for years and figured she could just go and ask one of her clients for a referral. She didn't heed my instructions to practice with at least three people. She stumbled over her words, skipped some steps, and felt ridiculous. She decided to practice.

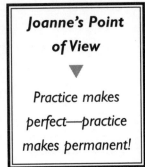

Joanne's Point of View

▼

Practice makes perfect—practice makes permanent!

ACTION STEP 19

More Practice

Plan to meet with two more people in the next week to practice.

Start Practicing

Asking for referrals is a new behavior. No matter how experienced you are, you need to practice. Practice the basics. Practice atTRACT so that the conversation just rolls off your tongue. You are genuine, caring, and compelling. You ask for what you want, and you get it!

Think about any major sports figure in baseball, basketball, or football. He practices the fundamentals.

- Why did Barry Bonds continue to take batting practice?
- Why did Rick Barry, the former great basketball player, never leave a basketball practice until he shot one hundred free throws and made at least ninety-two?
- Why did Jerry Rice practice his pass patterns over and over to make them crisp, sharp, and perfect?

Once you've practiced with three people, you'll be ready to go live. You will then set goals for how many people you will ask for referrals each and every week. As you begin to receive referrals, you will then track and measure your results. Referral selling will become habit, and you will increase your success rate exponentially.

Listen to the following story:

> There was a salesman being honored as Salesperson of the Year at a company celebration. The master of ceremonies asked this salesperson his secret to success. His answer: "I made one more call every day." He was ready to leave the office, had his jacket on, and picked up the phone and made one more call. He had carefully correlated the number of phone calls to the number of sales he made. You always have time for one more call, time to ask one more person for a referral, time to attend one more networking event.

> In baseball what separates a superior hitter from an average hitter is only thirty more hits in a season. That's all. While a .250 hitter is considered an average ballplayer, a .300 hitter is considered superior. If each of them has 600 at bats in a season, a .250 hitter will have 150 hits, while the .300 hitter will have 180 hits. The difference of only thirty hits equates to approximately one extra hit per week for an entire baseball season.

> This is the same kind of analysis you need to do for your business. How many additional "hits" do you need to get to reach your revenue and profit goals? How many more referral meetings and referral clients will get you to your goal? Get down to the fundamentals and practice. The more you ask, the more you get!

CHAPTER 11

The Responsibilities of Management: Get the Rocks Out of the Road

Whether you are a CEO, vice president, or sales manager, you have a central role in your company's sales process and in the decision to transition to referral selling. You are the sales leader. Referral selling is not just one more initiative to introduce to your organization. If you want to shift successfully to referral selling as a company, you must commit to the transition and let everyone know that you are becoming a referral-selling organization.

What this means is that everyone from the top down must do their part in generating referrals. You, the sales leader, will do what you ask others to do. And you will align all systems in your organization—recruiting, training, and compensation—to support the referral-selling process.

Above all, your job is to get the rocks out of the road for your salespeople so they can do what they were hired to do—sell!

Where Are You Now?

If salespeople were self-motivated, they wouldn't need managers or metrics. All of us perform our best when we are held accountable and have the tools to succeed. We don't respond to being told. We respond to being shown, recognized, and rewarded for successful behaviors.

We are the first to recognize a "program du jour." How many times has one of our executives read a book or spoken to a guru, and suddenly the entire organization is taking a new direction? As quickly as this new thinking evolves, it dies—replaced by yet another cutting-edge viewpoint or strategy. Unless you have carefully planned how you will shift to referral selling, you shouldn't be surprised if your announcement that your company is making a shift is greeted by, "Wait a minute, what happened to the other initiatives that used to be top priority?"

Please don't let this happen after reading this book. If you're not passionate about referral selling and committed to transforming your organization, please don't even consider starting the process. I want you to be successful and to have legions of prospects waiting to meet you. Increasing your revenue and profitability is a given. The real power of referral selling is that you will be working only with those clients you want to work with and who want to work with you—your Ideal Customers.

You, the executives, are the ones who will demonstrate your commitment to referral selling. Leaders do not ask others to do anything they would not do themselves. So your first action is to *show* your sales team your commitment. *You* need to do what you are asking them to do.

Making It Happen

Everyone in the organization has multiple roles to play in making the move to referral selling. There are organization practices, sales management practices, and individual practices that you must implement to ensure that referral selling becomes hard wired into the way you and your company work.

ORGANIZATION PRACTICES

The responsibility for implementing a major change always starts at the top. If the CEO or division head doesn't support the shift to referral selling, it's not going to happen. If you're the champion of this initiative, you need to get the CEO on board. Each and every executive must make the commitment. There can be no breaks in the chain of command, all the way down to the line managers—no "black holes" that will kill your shift to referral selling.

You've probably seen initiatives begun and then get stalled because handoffs were botched, or a manager gave his explicit agreement, but he didn't implicitly believe in the program. You've seen him sabotage a new initiative from the get-go by not holding people accountable for new behaviors and not shifting the way he runs his division or project.

To become a dynamic referral-selling organization, referral selling must become a priority. It cannot be an afterthought or something the organization does from time to time. It must become the way you work every day.

The good news is, once you have the right commitments, executing a referral strategy will be one of the easiest things you will ever do. Why? When your organization is focused on referral selling, everyone will be absolutely clear about the activities that are essential for success. Your decisions will be easy. A proposed project or a new business relationship will either get you to your goal or not. As new opportunities arise, you will be able to say yes or no on the spot.

Once you have the CEO and key sales executives on board, here are the steps you need to take:

1. Assess Your Sales Climate

How does your sales force really feel about selling? Here are some interview questions I use when I conduct presession meetings with my clients. Ask your sales team some of these questions and listen carefully to their answers. They are your front line and your ear to what is going on not only with your clients, but within your company.

Sales Team Questions

- Describe your perceptions of our sales culture.

    —What does the organization need to do more of, less of, or differently?

    —What does management/leadership need to do?

- How do you view your role in the sales process? What is working/not working for you in the sales effort?

  —Document specific areas to be commended.

  —Document specific obstacles, if any.

  —If you could change one or two specific things to improve the process, what would they be?

- What is working/not working in developing new clients? What do you see as the biggest obstacles—both organizationally and personally?

- What value do you receive from your manager?

- How confident are you that you will meet or exceed your revenue goals?

- How clear are you about what is expected of you?

- On a scale of 1 to 7, with 1 being poor and 7 being high, what is the level of client support you receive from your manager and senior executives?

- Are there things you would like to be doing that you're not doing?

- What advice do you think your customers would give to you?

- What else would you like to tell me that we haven't discussed?

Once you've conducted your interviews, compile your answers to these questions and document themes or trends. You will then be prepared to review your findings and determine which issues you want to tackle first.

2. Outline Your Sales Process

Have you created a clear and recognizable referral-selling process that everyone can understand and follow (see chapter 5)? Get your sales team together and test your process. What changes need to be made? Get their input for referral activities that should occur at each step. Remember, a sales process should not be complicated. It should be easy to follow and should include only those steps that will advance the sale and generate more referral business.

3. Create Company Metrics

At the beginning of your project, ask your clients how they will know when your initiative is successful. Determine the criteria that are important to the company and can easily be measured. Some referral metrics to consider are:

New Referral Customers: Decide how many additional referral customers your company plans to attract each week.

How will these customers translate into increases in revenue and profits? What additional products and services do you plan to cross-sell?

Customer Retention: Referral clients are more loyal and will be sources of additional referrals. Build a tracking system now that can measure your customer retention as it improves.

Salespeople Retention: When salespeople are no longer bogged down by cumbersome activities and are actually spending face time with their clients and making more deals, there is a marked shift in their attitude and morale. Referral-selling salespeople love their jobs!

Overall Employee Retention: In a referral-selling organization everyone is pulling together, and that means everyone can take credit for success. Employees are recognized and rewarded for their contribution to the company's success, and they will feel a renewed allegiance and enthusiasm. You will have created a loyalty that you never expected.

4. Clarify Roles and Responsibilities

Everyone in your organization is a part of the sales team, whether "sales" is in their titles or not. All employees know tons of people and should understand their roles in using their contacts to become Referral Sources for the organization. All you are asking is that they make introductions to your salespeople. You must dispel the concern that they are selling. This is a very real concern. If these people wanted to sell, they wouldn't be in their current jobs.

5. Align Reinforcement Systems

Consider a compensation plan for anyone who provides a referral. One of my clients instituted a plan that gives a 5 percent commission to anyone in the company who makes a referral that leads to a sale. Now that's a real incentive. You, as managers, must continue to encourage and orchestrate the almost infinite contact potential within your company. Devise a compensation plan to reward referral business—give a bonus or make a certain number of referral clients a ticket to an incentive trip. You will need to start rewarding all the activities that are part of referral selling.

6. Review Your New-Hire Program

Take a close look at your on-boarding process for all new hires, not just in sales. Everyone needs to know that they are expected to generate referrals for the organization. New hires need the technical know-how for their jobs as well as the skills and tools to become part of the referral team.

Here's what happens now: You hire salespeople; indoctrinate them with product knowledge; show them how to fill out time sheets, medical forms, and benefit forms; and give them a smattering of your business culture and the way you sell. Then you give them phones, lists, and desks, and expect them to figure out how to build their territory fast enough and well enough so that they can make the kind of money you promised them. You may think that because you are hiring experienced people, you don't need to train them. Think again. Every company has a different approach—not only to selling, but to other important disciplines.

When I worked for a banking consulting firm, many clients told us that they didn't need our credit training, as they were hiring experienced lenders. Within six months they came back to us, because they realized that every bank has a different way of doing a deal, spreading a cash-flow statement, and assessing risk. Experience is not a substitute for the way you do business. Train your new hires not only in what they do, but in how they do it. Get the rocks out of the road.

SALES MANAGEMENT PRACTICES

As a sales leader you have the day-to-day responsibility of keeping your team on track. Continue to reinforce and coach new selling behaviors so that referral selling becomes the way your salespeople work every day. Here are some key activities that will help you along the road:

Goal Setting

Create a specific referral-selling plan for your salespeople. How many people will they ask for referrals each week? How many referral meetings will they have? Each plan should be different based on what the salesperson can commit to accomplishing. The number doesn't matter as much as the commitment does. Each salesperson should have a plan to accomplish their referral activities each week.

Set clear expectations and realistic goals. People need to know what is expected of them and in what time frame. A goal is achievable with a little bit of stretch. We've all had goals that were so ridiculous that we just sat back and rolled our eyes. These kinds of goals are demotivating. Yes, expect your salespeople to excel, but don't make it impossible for them to do so.

Set revenue goals based on the average sale and the number of referrals and new clients you expect the salesperson to generate. As an example, assume that your average sale is $1.00. Your salesperson plans to ask eight people for referrals this month. Conservatively speaking, she gets only four referrals and closes two deals. That would mean a $2.00, or 100 percent, increase in revenue, plus two new clients.

Set goals for networking in the business and volunteer community. Determine which events and how many functions people should attend each week. Ensure that there is a way for people to share information with others after these events.

Accountability

Integrate referral-selling activities into your sales process, and hold people accountable for each step. Determine when people will ask for referrals and who will be asking. If you are targeting a current client and have many people working on a project, you cannot have everyone asking the same person for referrals. Strategize with your team and decide who asks whom. Within each client you will have multiple levels of contacts. Match the people with complementary relationships. In most cases you will match a CEO with a CEO, a VP with a VP, etc.

Rehearse

Ensure that people have clearly identified their Ideal Customer and are speaking in terms of business results. If they are not getting the traction you expected, it's time to rehearse. Role play an upcoming client interaction. What voicemail will they leave? Ask the question, "If you received this message, would you return the call?" What is their initial conversation? Most people resist practice, but it is critical to their success. It's one of the easiest things to do, takes minimal time, and has monumental results.

In a meeting with my clients, the CEO and the VP of sales at a major nonprofit organization, we reviewed the accomplishments of their sales team and discussed the next steps. One of my strong recommendations was for the salespeople to conduct a role-playing exercise of an upcoming client interaction during each sales meeting. The CEO immediately related to my suggestion, as he had formerly been the head of advertising for a major telecommunications company. He said that even experienced salespeople fall back on old habits. He told me that they used to do role-playing exercises at his previous company. He volunteered to attend upcoming sales meetings at the nonprofit and to play the customer role in order to sharpen the skills of his sales team.

Joint Call

Decide where your knowledge and influence could advance a sale, and become involved in the sales process. Years ago I was in a competitive situation with a potential client. It was going to be a tough battle. I knew the president of my company was the one who could swing the deal. Our presentation was on a Monday morning. The president was on the

East Coast and had to fly to California on a Sunday. He wanted to fly late in the day and arrive in the evening, as there was a big play-off basketball game that day. I said no, that we needed time to prepare for our presentation. We got the deal, so I think he eventually forgave me for ruining his weekend and his sports viewing.

Provide Feedback

Create opportunities for your sales team to learn and grow. Make sure that you give clear, immediate, and targeted feedback. Patting someone on the back and saying "great job" is not appropriate feedback. But telling salespeople that they did a great job of advancing the sale and then reviewing the insightful questions that they asked is reinforcing and motivating. Always state your observation of the behavior, and tell people specifically what they have done well. Do not mix motivational feedback with suggestions for improvement. People will be waiting for the other shoe to drop when you say, "Great job, but . . ." Ask your salespeople what they need to learn and grow, and then help them get what is needed.

Recognize and Reward Success

Put a plan in place to recognize successful referral activities. Proactively asking for referrals is a behavior change, and people may be uncomfortable doing it at first. When people meet their goals for asking for referrals, give them positive feedback and acclaim. Send group e-mail or voicemail messages when someone has been successful in getting a referral. Remember to include those in non-sales roles if they refer people who become clients.

Establish Individual Metrics

Measure the number of Referral Sources asked, number of referral meetings attended, number of new clients acquired, increases in revenue and profits made, cross-selling of products and services, and employee retention. Ensure that your database has a "Source" field to identify how a client was obtained. Continue to track and report referral results monthly. You should notice that the quality of your clients increases and the length of the sales cycle decreases.

Be sure to identify and monitor the essential referral activities that will get you to your revenue goal. Historically, sales have been tracked according to revenue only. Focus on referral-selling activities, and manage those.

Your results could be increases in revenue, additional business within existing clients, new client sales, or increases in deal profitability.

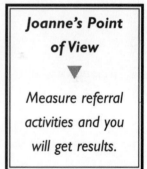

Joanne's Point of View

▼

Measure referral activities and you will get results.

Your role as sales manager is to get the rocks out of the road for your sales team. You need to pave the road internally and go to bat for them. Help your people navigate the internal politics and get to the right people, and help them externally by providing a cohesive strategy and clear goals.

You not only need to listen to your salespeople, but you

also need to take action. Salespeople have a bias for action, and they respect and are loyal to managers who act rather than promise. At my previous company, the president always had an open door and encouraged suggestions. Our salespeople met with him individually and in groups. He took copious notes and indicated that our suggestions were good ones. But then nothing ever happened. We were convinced that he put his copious notes in his desk drawer and never looked at them again. Finally, we gave up and decided that it was an exercise in futility to spend our time meeting with him. We said, "The heck with it," and implemented many ideas ourselves.

That's not how you want to run your organization. You don't want a bunch of renegade salespeople running around doing their own thing. Listen and take action. Tell your sales team what you will and will not do—and by when. One of my clients promised to introduce a mentoring program that would have given all new hires immediate answers and sales guidance. Months later, the program still had not been introduced.

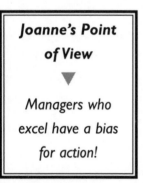

Joanne's Point of View

▼

Managers who excel have a bias for action!

Their salespeople called me to ask what was going on. I was the one who went to the sales executive to let him know that his team felt they were being left out to dry. Within two weeks the program was launched. Take action and do what you say you're going to do, and your sales team will trust you and will thrive.

Individual Practices

Ultimately, you'll want everyone in the organization to be involved in creating referrals. From the beginning of your transition to a referral-selling organization, it will be absolutely essential for management to demonstrate their individual commitment to the Referral-Selling System. How terrific is it when both the CEO and a junior new hire can be in the corporate newsletter as having played a part in helping to create referral sales!

What are you, the executive, going to do to generate referrals? You have a myriad of contacts that I bet could use some nurturing. You need to follow the same process as your salespeople.

Build your Referral Wheel with at least one hundred names, and set goals around how many people you will contact each week.

Attend and participate in networking events and professional organizations. Set goals for the number of events you will attend each week. Help your sales team identify the professional organizations that are the best for their business. There are so many options that people often don't know where to go. Your approach to attending different organization events should be strategic. Where do your clients go? What are the industry groups that support your vertical markets? You might decide to have a divide-and-conquer strategy—assign different salespeople to different organizations. Be sure they share what they've learned with your entire team.

Obtain an introduction to your referrals. Once you receive a referral, have been introduced, and have scheduled a meeting with the prospect, determine what role you will play in this ongoing relationship. You need to decide how many people will manage this relationship with the new client, and on the first meeting you will want to bring your lead person along. This is your relationship, so you need to make your contact feel comfortable. You will want to have some level of involvement going forward.

Leverage your contacts within your community plus your business relationships. You have senior contacts and relationships that your salespeople don't. You can open many doors for them. Think about the volunteer work you do, the charities you support, the events you go to with your kids, or your golfing buddies.

ACTION STEP 20

Management Practices

- Determine your organization, sales management, and individual best practices.
- Talk to your sales team, and take action on their recommendations.

What It Takes to Get from Here to There (You Can Do It!)

Commitment

I was in a meeting recently with a potential client. One of the partners, George, looked at me and asked a pointed question. He wanted to know if he could speak to one of my other clients in his industry to discuss the results they achieved with my Referral-Selling System. I told him that my other client would report that the workshop was fabulous. Everyone loved

Management Practices Checklist

▼

Organization Practices	❑ Assess sales climate ❑ Outline sales process ❑ Create company metrics ❑ Clarify roles and responsibilities ❑ Align reinforcement systems ❑ Review new-hire program
Sales Management Practices	❑ Set goals ❑ Establish accountability ❑ Rehearse ❑ Conduct joint calls ❑ Provide feedback ❑ Recognize and reward success ❑ Establish individual metrics
Individual Practices	❑ Build your Referral Wheel ❑ Attend networking events and professional organizations ❑ Obtain an introduction to referrals ❑ Leverage your contacts

it and took away lots of tips and tools. However, management was not committed to executing the process. It was all lip service. A big part of the problem was that senior management was still asking people to cold call. They had "blitz nights" during which they called current customers to cross-sell other services. One of my workshop participants was totally discouraged. He said, "Why did they send us to training on referral skills when they are still asking us to cold call?" He threw up his hands in disgust. The message and the execution were out of sync.

George thanked me for being honest and then admitted that his management team would have the same problem. They needed to make referral selling a priority—for themselves as well as for their salespeople. He looked at me and said, "Would you be willing to come in and meet with us on a quarterly basis to keep us on track?" With that question, I knew this was my Ideal Customer. The management team was willing to commit both the time and resources to change the way they worked.

EXECUTION

We can have the best intentions and the best plans, but if we can't execute, it's not only a waste of time, but it's demoralizing for our employees. You need to show your company that referral selling is now the way you work. It is your methodology, and you will track, measure, and reward results. You've paved the way for your company's success!

Training itself will not produce results. Telling others what to do will not produce results. Only an uncompromising commitment by sales executives and business owners to a new way of working will provide an increase in both revenue and profits.

If you're not committed to transforming your organization, please don't even consider starting the process. You, the executives, are the ones who will demonstrate your commitment to referral selling not just by saying it, but by modeling it and changing your reinforcement structure. You, too, need to be believers in the Referral-Selling System.

CHAPTER 12

Selling Bells and Whistles or the Whole Train?

I once owned a luggage and gift store. My easiest sales were made when people were buying small luxuries for themselves. When I would put a soft, exquisite, fragrant Italian leather wallet in their hands, there was often an immediate love affair. The product sold itself. The customers did all the work of translating the features (soft Italian leather, slim, beautiful stitching, great color) and benefits (makes me feel good, will impress others) to results and return on investment (ROI) (people will like me more, my clients will be impressed with my good taste and will bring me more business). For me as a salesperson, it was great. All I had to do was stand there and agree.

In the real world where much more sophisticated demands are made on sales professionals, all too many salespeople are still talking in terms of features and benefits, or bells and whistles, while buyers want to hear about the things they actually need, like having their goods delivered on time. Buyers don't want to hear about bells and whistles anymore—they want the whole train. They need to know how you are going to improve their business results and want you to measure those results in terms of ROI. For salespeople, the bar has been raised. You must become at least as sophisticated as your clients.

Those salespeople who are closing deals are the ones who prove the business results their product or service delivers. When possible, they are translating those results into ROI, because the only thing customers care about is whether their investment is going to pay for itself time and time again in terms of increased revenue, profits, employee loyalty, or customer loyalty.

Recent research by Real Learning (www.reallearning.com) about why executives buy issues a caution for salespeople to step back and see if they are equipped to sell business results to the CXO level.

- Executives say that their purchasing decisions are influenced by whether the purchase will quickly help them improve customer satisfaction, achieve operational excellence, or get and keep the right people.
- Executives do not focus on product features or even on solving particular business problems. Executives do look to salespeople to help them navigate the swiftly flowing waters of change. Salespeople who directly link their products and services to positive business results are the salespeople who get these executives' business.
- The challenge of selling to executives is further

complicated by the short planning horizon companies now maintain. Executives report that on average, long-term planning means just twenty months out. Short-term planning covers six months. Purchases and other decisions must deliver results within those time frames, or they won't even be considered.

Wow! We have our work cut out for us. We not only have to deliver business results and an ROI, but we need to deliver them in six to twenty months.

Many times we may wonder why clients delay buying decisions or don't have much of a response when we present what is clear to us is a perfect solution. We wonder, "What's going on?" You need to look at how you were presenting. Were you talking in terms of features and benefits or results and ROI?

Selling Results

George Papa, senior vice president of Altera Corporation (www.altera.com), says that he will listen to a salesperson who has taken the time to find out about his needs and the problems he is trying to solve. These good salespeople are the ones who add value and propose a relevant solution. According to Papa, most salespeople (85 percent) simply push their products. They're focused solely on their own need to sell and don't demonstrate either the patience or the skills to develop and close a complex sale. If that 85 percent doesn't see an immediate return, they lose patience, get discouraged, and drop the ball.

George related a story about a company we'll call Dyna-Blast that sold explosives. Its product (dynamite) had become a commodity, and customers, reasonably enough, made purchases based on price. DynaBlast was getting squeezed on price, and its profits were shrinking. One of its largest clients dynamited rocks. Once DynaBlast's salespeople began asking probing questions about their client's business problems, they learned that the client wanted to get more of a specific size stone from a single blast. Based on this new information, DynaBlast developed a stick of dynamite that gave the client more stones of the size and shape it wanted in each blast, which significantly reduced the client's costs. The DynaBlast salespeople had identified the real business problem and had delivered the right solution. As a result, their client chose DynaBlast as their preferred supplier. And because they delivered a measurable business result, DynaBlast got themselves out of the commodity business and into the solutions business. Now it can sell its dynamite at a price based on its value to the customer, which is nearly twice what it could get before.

In spite of this strong empirical evidence and impartial research, clients (even salespeople who've been selling for years) consistently tell me that they've slid backwards into talking about features. The attraction is that it's easy. Now is the time to forget about features—the key characteristics of your product. Whether it's a special device on your vacuum cleaner (your customer wants to know that it will save two hours a week in housework) or the liquid cooling that makes your computer quieter than your competitor's (delivering 20 percent higher productivity in a quiet environment), you've got to let go of features and start thinking about and selling what your product does for your client—the dollar value.

There are only two ways to talk about results—the actual business results and the ROI your product or service delivers. We are in a service economy, so chances are you're selling services, and the challenge is even greater. It's more difficult to talk about business results and ROI when you are selling services than when you are selling tangible products. You need to make the translation from the intangible (the service) to the tangible (business results or ROI).

From now on we're only going to talk about results or ROI. Let's review the definitions:

Business results are the actual quantitative changes that clients expect to see in their business. For consumers the result is an improved aspect of their lives. For a business the result is a better way of getting something done— an improvement in a business process, sales, profitability, conversion rate of prospects to clients, or retention of key employees. The client will be able to monitor and measure the impact from your product and will know when and what results have been achieved.

ROI compares the dollar value of business results to the investment your client has made. For example, a dollar spent on this system today will return $10 to the bottom line in one year.

What interests clients the most? Results! Why do they buy? ROI. How are we taught? Features! How many of us learned how to have an ROI discussion in boot camp? Very few. That discussion, if it occurred at all, came later—when you had more experience with the company and had already learned the ropes.

I recently facilitated a global sales meeting for a technology company in the Silicon Valley. My charter was to focus the sales team on acquiring new clients by developing and then communicating the company's value proposition (business results) to its target clients. To do this the salespeople needed to approach their products from an entirely different perspective.

I divided the participants into product groups, and their assignment was to answer the following questions: Who was their Ideal Customer, what were the business issues of their buyer, what were the pain points, what were anticipated objections, what questions should they ask, what was a deal breaker, what had been typical business results for this kind of client in the past, and who would be the Referral Source to this client in the future? Each group then created a value proposition and sample questions for one of their target clients.

One group invited their product manager to participate in the discussion. They questioned her intensely—not about the features of the product but about how they should sell it. Although the product had been launched, it was clear that the salespeople did not yet understand the product well enough to sell it. They didn't know the questions to ask or their competition, and most importantly, they couldn't articulate their value proposition.

As a result of the meeting, salespeople were armed with their most valuable tool—a clear and compelling ROI proposition to deliver to their clients. They were not only able to secure new appointments with their target buyers, but the conversion rate of prospects to customers shot up from 25 percent to over 50 percent. Their cost of sales plummeted, because salespeople were now getting meetings with the right people and were no longer wasting valuable technical resources chasing unqualified prospects.

The "So What?" Factor

Our job as salespeople is to connect the dots from the products or services that we provide to actual business results and, ultimately, to ROI. It's not our customers' job. We won't make the sale unless we provide the links between our offerings and the business results expressed as ROI that we can deliver to our clients. If your client can say, "So what?" you haven't nailed the business result.

If you talk about features, you can't answer the "So what?" question. Take the example of a table in a restaurant. It has four legs, is round, and has a plastic laminate (Formica) top. These are features. So what? What is the business result that the table actually provides you? Take the same table and talk about results: The legs are recessed, so your restaurant customers won't hit their shins and get bruises, and therefore are more likely to enjoy their meal and return; the table is round, so there are no corners to bang people in the hips (see result from recessed legs), and you can use smaller tablecloths, reducing your laundry bill by 20 percent. The Formica top means faster cleanup than your previous wood tops, reducing busboy time by 15 percent and increasing table turnover by 15 percent. And for each of these you can provide a specific dollar value, based on the customer's existing costs. You *can* answer the "So what?" question when you talk about results—you are crystal clear about what the table does for you.

Think about what your clients have told you they have achieved by working with you. How is their business different than it would have been? What has been the bottom-line impact? Have they saved time or money? Have they improved some important aspect of their lives (less travel or fewer emergencies at work)? Remember to quantify the results.

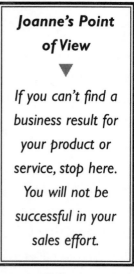

Joanne's Point of View

▼

If you can't find a business result for your product or service, stop here. You will not be successful in your sales effort.

I was working with investment advisors from a large financial services firm. When I asked them to translate their service into business results, they had a very difficult time. The managers said that what I was asking them to do was extremely important but very tough.

We began by getting rid of the many "touchy-feely" statements they had been using: "We help you achieve your financial dream." "We can put your mind at rest." "We can help you achieve your financial goals." Everyone makes these statements, and they're not business results. (Remember, if you can say, "So what?" it is not a result.) After considerable effort, the group proffered a few really good results statements that caught my attention:

- The assets in your portfolio will continue to grow. (They substantiated this statement with third-party research about the performance of their portfolios.)
- You will be able to send your children to college.
- You will be able to buy that vacation home you thought was unattainable.
- You will be able to retire with the security you want.

Because they were now able to communicate specific, powerful results, their referrals increased, and their business began to accelerate.

Maybe It's Not So Tough After All

When you are referred, you already have a business case ally in the form of your Referral Source. If a Referral Source is able to say, as part of the referral, that the bottom-line impact your solution or product had was positive, that's a powerful start to a good business discussion. It establishes your credibility right out of the box. If your Referral Sources don't have an ROI success story from doing business with you, then you need to furnish them with an ROI account from a result you produced elsewhere that can be related to others. That will be almost as good as having had the experience themselves.

It is much easier to ask for a referral when you have a strong business case. You are respecting your Referral Source by giving him concrete examples to share with others. Likewise, you are getting more respect from your Referral Source, because you have clearly communicated the business results his contacts can expect. Referral selling is high quality and higher-level selling, and it demands more than bells and whistles. Talking about bells and whistles is low-level selling. It reduces you and your offering to the lowest common denominator—a commodity—and you will lose the price war. If you want to get the most out of referral selling, you need a strong business case.

Here are examples of how some businesses have demonstrated their business results:

CPA Firm: A CPA firm selling to high-net-worth individuals showed that they could save their clients tax dollars, would stay on top of the latest laws, and would make sure their clients were not hit with penalties because of changes in the law. They also helped their clients take advantage of new tax-reduction opportunities.

Website Construction: Linda Gold, president of M3iworks (www.m3iworks.com), says that clients want three things: 1) top quality, 2) vendor integrity and reliability (guaranteed pricing, delivery, responsiveness, and satisfaction), and 3) the lowest price. She tells her clients they can only have two, so they need to make the choice. You can't have "best," "fast," and "cheap" at the same time. As far as her websites go, Linda says that if you want a website that attracts customers, converts them into buying customers, and builds ongoing loyalty, then the highest ROI will come from the first and the second items. Because her company provides ongoing service, she can demonstrate that many of her current clients are realizing at least a 50 percent savings over what they had previously been paying for full-time staff to maintain and upgrade their websites.

Long-Term-Care Insurance: Most people work extremely hard to build their assets for retirement. Louis Brownstone, chairman of California Long Term Care Insurance Services (www.californialongtermcare.com), shows how these assets can disappear in a blink with the astronomical costs of health care, and how long-term-care insurance will protect assets from being depleted. Brownstone demonstrates that the right insurance will relieve the financial and emotional burden of care from your family and even enable you to be cared for in your own home.

Automobile Insurance: Most consumers consider automobile insurance a commodity, but Mark Williams, area manager for the California State Automobile Association (www.csaa.com), establishes that this couldn't be further from the truth. Mark shows his customers that lower prices almost always mean more exclusions and exceptions, and, ultimately, poorer results when trying to settle claims. As an example, he shows that many people are paying too much for basic comprehensive and collision insurance. Those same dollars could be used to increase coverage for medical and uninsured motorists—areas where drivers have the most liability. If you cause an accident and hurt someone, and the other driver is seriously injured, your personal assets could be at stake if you don't have proper coverage.

Financial Advisor: How does one financial advisor justify the fees for comprehensive financial advice? She guarantees that her clients will make more than her fee. She shows her clients the dollars-and-cents cost of advice and compares it to the consequences of not receiving advice. She reviews her historical performance and demonstrates the results as an example of what a new client can expect. She also points out the value in peace of mind: Her clients know that someone else is worrying about their retirement, so they can sleep at 3 A.M.

Realtor: A Realtor can demonstrate that her clients will never overpay for a property and will get it at the right price. Clients will only preview properties that meet their criteria. The Realtor will be the first to point out problems with a property, such as an unsafe location, deferred maintenance, inability to expand, and a low margin for appreciation.

Training Company: Suzanne Saxe, former president and CEO of Advance Consulting (www.advanceconsulting.com), asks her clients how they want to measure success. Advance Consulting is a professional development company that helps technical and functional experts transform themselves into consultants and business partners. Typical metrics that her clients value are increases in revenue, customer satisfaction, and employee productivity. Suzanne is able to tell her referrers that Advance Consulting's clients usually agree that 25 percent of their increases can be attributed to Advance's training.

Your Biggest Competitor

If you can't demonstrate business results easily, you can talk about the consequences of *not* moving forward, including overlooked opportunities and unforseen business losses. As an example, if a CPA firm has a client that is launching an international business, they can point out the results of not fully investigating the tax consequences of headquartering in various alternate states. For even a medium-sized firm, that can quickly run into millions of dollars.

Talk about the consequences of *not* using your service. Inertia is often the most formidable competitor we have. Demonstrate why the client can't afford to delay a decision. Show the lack of results—or even worse, the demise of the entire enterprise.

In the late 1980s when I worked in the banking industry, our product that taught lenders how to make commercial loans sold for almost $700 per user. That seemed like a lot of money in those days. A banker's job is to assess risk, and banking management is concerned about making bad loans. Bankers are equally concerned about discovering that a loan is in trouble only when it is too late to save it. If the first time a banker realizes a company is in trouble is when he sees a bad financial statement, it is already too late. The loan has "gone south." Our training taught bankers how to recognize the early warning signs long before they showed up on a financial statement. When bank executives would push back on the price for our product, I would say, "What is one bad loan worth to you?" It was always way more than $700.

A data storage company has a compelling case for talking about inertia. Its clients cannot risk maintaining the status quo. When clients are running mission-critical applications, the recovery time must be instantaneous. If a system goes down, the business impact can be millions of dollars in lost revenue, plus massive customer defection. The cost of waiting to implement enterprise data storage can be catastrophic. So when a data storage company is selling, it needs to sell directly against the enormous potential cost of doing nothing.

ACTION STEP 21

Results and ROI Worksheet

Complete the Results column of the Results and ROI worksheet (see p. 193) for your Ideal Customer.

Return on Investment

Developing an ROI analysis takes some concentrated work. Every industry has its unique challenges, so find out what you require from your company in order to have an ROI discussion with your client. Then start building your case. This is one of the most important tasks you will undertake as a sales professional, and it's urgent!

Clarify and get agreement with your client on the criteria for a successful project before you ever begin. Ensure that you can justify your ROI. As an example, if you are selling software, clients may tell you that they will have justified the expenditure if productivity can be increased by a minimum of 20 percent. You now know the result that is required by your

Results and ROI

▼

Ideal Customer's Business Issues	Business Results	ROI

client, and you can put the people, processes, and products in place to ensure success.

Here are some ROI examples from a variety of businesses:

Long-Term-Care Insurance: More than half of all women and a third of all men who live to age sixty-five will spend time in a nursing home before they die (*Wall Street Journal,* February 21, 2000). At an inflation rate of 5 percent, the annual average cost of nursing home care will grow to over $330,000 in twenty years and will exceed $540,000 in thirty years. No matter what your age, it is unlikely that you will ever pay more in total premiums for long-term-care insurance over your lifetime than you would pay for a one-year stay in a nursing home.

Data Storage Company: A data storage company automates the storage of mission-critical data. Its clients have typically had an expensive downtime event, need to hire additional storage administrators, need to avoid additional storage purchases, or have grown or acquired companies and thus have new storage needs. There are actually four ROI factors that this company's salespeople can calculate:

- Reduce staffing costs: Once reports become automated, the storage administrator's time is freed up, and the need to hire additional resources is eliminated.

- Reduce hardware costs: Automating the storage process improves the efficiency of existing hardware and eliminates the need to purchase additional equipment.

- Reduce downtime: Automating the process reduces

the chances for applications to fail and at the same time provides faster problem diagnosis. For ROI purposes downtime must be expressed in hours and days, and faster diagnosis in time, personnel, and dollars.

- Increase business agility: Automation speeds up business processes and allows an IT department to respond quickly to requests. Again, ROI should be expressed in time, personnel, and dollars saved.

Employee Retention Company: The actual cost of a salesperson leaving a company can be astronomical, according to B. Lynn Ware, president and CEO of Integral Talent Systems (ITS) (www.itsinc.net). For them it's easy to measure the ROI for their clients by demonstrating the dollar consequences of *not* investing in the retention of their top salespeople. When salespeople leave, for instance, ITS can show companies that they will be faced with 1) the cost of hiring a new employee, which is one and a half times the employee's future yearly salary, plus benefits; 2) the loss of productivity once the salesperson has decided to leave; 3) the cost of recruiting; 4) the possible loss of competitive knowledge once a prized employee goes over the wall to the competition; 5) the humongous danger that the best of that person's team will follow; 6) the loss of productivity until the new people are fully integrated and up to speed; and 7) the loss of sales opportunities and clients while the territory goes uncovered. ITS shows that $1 spent on retention can save $50 in turnover costs.

Incentive Travel Company: Justifying the expenditure and ROI for an incentive program for salespeople and their clients can be difficult. How do you measure ROI on something as soft as a sales-incentive program? By measuring client retention as well as the number of new clients the company attracts within six months after the program.

If a client who has been on an incentive trip has a choice between buying your product and a similar product from another company, can you demonstrate a bottom-line result? Susan Alpert, president of International Travel Incentives in Santa Ana, California (www.intltravelincentives.com), says customers will do everything in their power to buy from her clients, who reward both clients and salespeople with elegant, tasteful, and exotic trips. None of their competitors can match these experiences. New hires, salespeople, and clients ask what trip is being offered for the upcoming year, and then they make buying decisions based on the destination. The trips actually drive behavior. The ROI is the amount of new revenue minus the cost of the trip.

Conversion Time

Now it's time to convert your business results into a return on investment. Even if your client never asks, you will be steps ahead if you are prepared to have an ROI discussion. The only way you can calculate ROI is if you can quantify the results. Do a calculation for one of your previous engagements or develop a scenario that you can share with clients. Calculate the savings or additional earnings your client will receive, and divide by the cost to your client for your product or services. You will then get his ROI. Then you can say, "Typically, my clients achieve an *x* percent return on their investment with us."

ACTION STEP 22

Compute Your ROI

Complete the ROI column of the Results and ROI worksheet (see p. 193) for your Ideal Customer.

Here is an ROI example of a sales team transitioning to referral selling. I typically plot an extremely conservative example, which I base on my client's business. They can then envision what their new selling world will look like. I have converted the intangible (Referral-Selling System) to the tangible (business results and ROI). A company has ten salespeople, and the value of a typical average annual sale is $10,000. Let's say that as a result of implementing a referral-selling strategy, each salesperson will have one additional sale per year. The client will thus recognize an increase of $10,000 per salesperson (average sale), or $100,000 for the entire team ($10,000 x 10 = $100,000). The cost of converting to referral selling is the cost of training ten people, plus implementing a referral-selling process ($25,000). Their ROI is thus three times the cost (a $25,000 investment results in a net result of $75,000 in additional revenue). That's a 300 percent ROI!

This example is so powerful that it typically closes the deal. When I meet a real "numbers" guy, I will offer to demonstrate my ROI worksheet. This was the case with a sales manager at an alarm company. Most alarm companies have an atypical business model. They lose money on the installation of a system, but they make money on their service contracts. They have a renewable service that clients won't change unless they have a particularly bad experience.

The client and I walked through my ROI example using a basic retail installation—their least expensive service—approximately $100 in 2003. We made two conservative assumptions about converting to a referral-selling methodology: Each salesperson would increase his referral business by 15 percent, and this referral business would have a 60 percent close rate. The net-net gain to the organization after three years, after factoring in the cost of client acquisition and the cost of salespeople, was close to $300,000. The ROI was over 500 percent. And that was for the lowest cost alarm service. The client said that if my calculations worked for their screwy business model, they would work for anyone.

If you'd like to see what an ROI worksheet looks like, visit my website at www.nomorecoldcalling.com/tools and review what I provide for my clients to demonstrate the bottom-line results from transitioning to referral selling. You can then develop your own ROI worksheet based on this one.

Getting Help

How do you find the answers to all of your business results and ROI questions? Turn first to your marketing department and product managers. They may not always understand what you need, so be clear about what information is important to you in order to sell your service.

One of my colleagues began a new job as marketing manager for a major health insurance company. Her charter was to set the strategy for launching several new products. Her boss, an operations guy, gave her a binder and told her to figure it out. When she asked to speak to their insurance brokers, she was told that it wasn't necessary. She forged ahead on her own by finding mentors to help her navigate the internal politics to get the information she needed without visibly going around her boss. She built a business case for talking to the brokers to uncover what they needed. As a result, she was able to help her company develop the business results and ROI numbers that made possible a successful launch of their new product.

If you are a marketing professional, spend time with your sales force. Talk to them, call on clients with them, ask what they need from you to be successful at referral selling, and then deliver. Your salespeople will love you.

Salespeople need to know the following:

- The Ideal Customer for your product. To whom should they be referred?
- The business issue the product solves. What is the

business case they can share with their Referral
Source?

- The success cases with hard ROI numbers. What are
  easy ways to demonstrate ROI to their Referral
  Source?
- The questions to qualify this customer. What are the
  essential questions they can prompt their Referral
  Source to ask?
- The sales cycle and delivery for the product. Is this a
  proven solution or a new offering? If it is a new offering, what are the anticipated business results?

Test Your Assumptions

It's now time to give your assumptions about business results
and ROI a reality check. Test your business case with your
peers and your Business Buddy. If you are a sales manager,
schedule a sales meeting to brainstorm different ROI scenarios.
Ask someone to be the person who asks, "So what?" Remember, if you can say "So what?" you have not communicated
business results or ROI.

ACTION STEP 23

ROI Testing

- Test your assumptions with your Business Buddy and a client.
- Carry the chart around with you and review it often. Keep it by your phone, in your car, and in your briefcase.

Continue to question, qualify, and test your assumptions. Carefully study and use your business results and ROI examples. You will no longer be on the commodity train. You'll no longer be talking about bells and whistles. You'll be helping your clients make significant changes that impact their businesses. They will now be thanking you. Get on the ROI train before it leaves the station, and have a great ride! Ding ding. Toot toot.

CHAPTER 13

Red Flags: Before You Hit the Panic Button

What If . . . ?

You may recall that the road to Oz was interrupted by the occasional surprise, such as nasty flying monkeys and seductive fields of opium poppies. Although I've attempted to make the road to referral selling as smooth as possible, years of experience have taught me that there can be bumps in it. Here are some red flags to give you an early alert that something may not be going as well as it ought to and what to do about it before it becomes a big problem.

WHAT IF THEY DON'T CALL BACK?

We discussed the fact that when you've been introduced to prospects, they will always return your calls. However, you may be getting frustrated and irritated because you haven't heard back. People are really busy, so you need to be patient and persistent. Send an e-mail follow-up with "Referred by" in the subject line. Wait a week and call again. If you still don't get a call back, check in with your Referral Source and ask for her help. Your Referral Source may tell you that the contact is on vacation, had a new baby, married off her daughter, or is going through a massive reorganization at work. When one of my clients went back to his Referral Source, he learned that the contact had been in the hospital, and it would probably be another week or so before a meeting could be scheduled. End result: My client could now plan how to spend his time, and he got the meeting a week later.

WHAT IF YOUR REFERRAL SOURCE CAN'T THINK OF ANYONE?

Be specific. It's so easy to say, "If you know anyone who could benefit from my services, please let them know about me." Whew, you've said it and checked it off your list. You've asked. And you feel even better if your contact asks for your business card. The reality is you're not in any better position than if you hadn't asked at all. All you've done is checked "asking for a referral" off your list. You need to take the time to clearly describe your Ideal Customer. Remember, you are like an artist. The more color and lines you put in your picture, the easier it will be for your Referral Source to think of the perfect referral for you.

One of my banker clients decided to focus on the commercial real estate market, and he asked a current client for a referral. Bankers have an additional concern about asking for referrals: If a customer is referred to them and the bank can't do the deal, both the banker and the Referral Source have the potential to be embarrassed. Bankers really need to be specific in describing their Ideal Customer. So now my client not only asks for a commercial real estate customer, he gives his Referral Source three other criteria: The company needs to have been in business for at least three years, have a positive cash flow, and have a growing enterprise. He has now increased his chances exponentially of getting introduced to a bankable customer.

If you are asking for referrals and getting a lot of people saying that they can't think of anyone at the moment, go back to see if you are being specific enough. And, you can help jog their memories by reviewing several categories of potential contacts from the Referral Wheel—perhaps a neighbor, a business associate, or a member of their professional group could be an ideal referral for you.

What If You've Just Moved to a New Town?

A salesperson moved from Los Angeles to New York and began working for a new company. He didn't have a personal network in New York. How could he build a referral business? Jeff Meleski of Communispace Corp. (www.communispace .com) was just that person. Not only did he move 3,000 miles away, but he joined a company that had limited brand awareness in his market. Jeff committed to building his business through referrals. By using the atTRACT process, he quickly identified his Ideal Customer and set a goal for asking for referrals. He leveraged the few personal relationships and acquaintances he had to build a referral stream that is working for him to identify leads as well as to connect him with additional professional contacts.

As a result, within just thirty days, Jeff increased his qualified sales pipeline situations by 50 percent. He's continuing to network, and he's increased his Referral Sources by more than 30 percent. He's still new to the market, but Jeff says that working your geography with purpose and diligence makes all the difference in how quickly you can build your business.

What If Your Boss Tells You to Stick with a Proven System?

You are ready to transition to referral selling, but your boss tells you to cold call and to follow up on incoming leads. You are held accountable for making a certain number of dials each day. What should you do? Work with your existing customers, and ask them for referrals. Review your Referral Wheel, and identify key people you could ask. Remember, it's not about who they are, it's about the people they know. And you don't know whom they know until you ask. As you begin to locate qualified leads and convert them to sales, your boss will begin to notice your success. Your goal will be to gradually transition to referral selling by spending more and more time with referral business and less and less time on unproductive prospecting techniques.

What If You're Transitioning to Referral Selling and You're Not Seeing the Results You Expected?

What is your Transition Management Plan? It's not a straight line between where you are now and where you want to go. The shift to referral selling is a major transition—you are changing the way you and your organization work. Any change process requires strong sponsorship on many levels, a plan to anticipate and uncover resistance, adequate skills to do the new task, and alignment with company and individual values. Many managers think that change will just happen when they announce it, and that the organization will begin to operate in a new way. Because they fail to prepare people and to get everyone on board, the initiative hits many bumps, can easily derail, and can become another "program du jour."

However, when you invest time and resources up front and have a plan in place to address typical resistance and decreases in productivity during the transition, you will get faster results. Your transition costs will be lower, and your organization will be operating at a higher level of productivity than when you started.

Are there consequences to not completing the transition? What are the consequences if you don't keep your commitment to referral selling—whether you are a manager or an individual contributor? If there's no downside, then you really don't have an impetus to change. Will you make less money, be fired, go out of business, or lose the good customers you already have? Take a close look and decide if you've really bought into the referral-selling process.

One of my clients faced this same quandary about its transition to referral selling. We thought that we had addressed the company's challenges and enumerated the changes required in the transition. Here's what actually happened:

- **Took Longer:** The time to ramp up took longer than anyone expected. Many people thought that the best and biggest accomplishments would occur immediately after training—when everyone was on board, had the tools, and was excited. Actually, the opposite is true. The best results occur after people have had time to practice and become comfortable with their new skills.

• **Manager Overload:** The managers who had participated in the pilot were assigned another major project just a few weeks later. Managers were being pulled in too many directions without having clear priorities.

• **Change Process:** The shift to referral selling was indeed a major implementation challenge. The switch was changing the way people were selling. In addition to the referral initiative, there had just been a major reorganization, and salespeople were put into new roles with different responsibilities.

• **Resistance:** Participants appeared "bought in." They agreed that referrals were the only way to work, but they didn't take the time to practice and build their skills. They said the right words, but they were just as happy to work the way they always had—the way they were comfortable.

• **Consequences:** There were really no major consequences for not getting referrals. Yes, their compensation could decrease, but they wouldn't lose their jobs.

• **Accountability:** Managers agreed to hold their people accountable for five referral requests per week. Each manager received a checklist of follow-up activities. However, because of other demands, they did not set goals with their people, coach them on the atTRACT process, or set the expectation that they would all be working in a new way. In addition, they did not follow the process themselves after they had made commitments to ask for referrals. They were asking their people to do what they were not willing to do. Managers did not follow up on the assignment of Business Buddies, and so another opportunity for practice and feedback was lost.

• **Sponsorship:** Senior management agreed in principle about referral selling, but they did not realize the implications of this change and the fact that people were dealing with a new organization, new roles, and many other competing initiatives.

What to do? We decided to do a midcourse correction. My client met with the senior line manager to align priorities. He also met again with the managers in the pilot, and they agreed to re-sponsor themselves and to commit to referral goals both for themselves and for their teams. We determined that after the pilot, we would undertake these additional steps for the rollout:

- Select the rollout groups based on individual managers' strengths and commitments.
- Introduce a "Transition to Referral Selling" module for all managers as part of the launch of the referral initiative.
- Have managers set the context with their teams and get "buy-in."
- Recalibrate metrics that were adjusted for the ramp-up time.

Recognize that the transition to referral selling is a change process. Take a close look at your organizational processes and individual commitment. Anticipate and plan for the change, and determine how it will impact your organization. Monitor your plan closely, and make adjustments as they are needed along the way.

WHAT IF EVERYONE SAYS THEY'RE TOO BUSY?

I've never heard anyone say that they had so much time on their hands that they didn't know what to do with all of it. Everyone is busy. So I don't buy the excuse that you are too busy to ask for referrals. The time you should be asking is when you have the most contact with your customers. Make the time. Asking for referrals must become part of your sales process—you must integrate it into the work you do every day. One of my clients, a manager at a major brokerage firm, integrated asking for referrals into the customer-service calls she made. The more she asked, the more she was supercharged. Customers began giving her wonderful referrals, and she couldn't wait until the next call to ask again.

WHAT IF YOU TRIED ASKING, BUT IT HASN'T WORKED?

Review the atTRACT process. Are you following the process, or are you taking some shortcuts? As you become more comfortable with and fluent in asking for referrals, you may inadvertently shortcut the process by not making it clear that you build your business through referrals, not specifically describing your Ideal Customer, or not asking for the introduction. You may rush conversations and not give others the opportunity to help you. You may revert to begging and pleading questions instead of coming right out and asking for what you want.

One of my clients called me to get feedback on her atTRACT conversations. She sells long-term-care insurance and had been calling her previous clients to ask for referrals and to offer a new service—a review of their life insurance policies— to make sure that they were not over- or under-insured. My client was purposeful and strong in her offer to review the insurance policy, but when she asked for a referral, she stumbled over her words and was not clear about what she needed. When she refocused on the needs of her Ideal Customers, clarified her strong business case for them, and was passionate about asking for referrals, she not only got the appointment but she also got referrals!

Always remember that you are the expert and are great at what you do. You need to ask for referrals from a position of strength—no begging and pleading.

WHAT IF YOU'RE STILL HAVING DIFFICULTY?

- Go to this special page on my website with top tips for all of my No More Cold Calling graduates: www.nomorecoldcalling.com/toptips/. These short tips should be good memory joggers for you. Many have found the help they were looking for right there.
- Connect with your Business Buddy. Be sure to stay in touch and hold each other accountable. Your key activity should be to set goals with each other for the num-

ber of people and the names of people you will ask for referrals in the upcoming week. Practice a couple of sample conversations, and give productive and honest feedback to each other.

• Send an e-mail to joanne@nomorecoldcalling.com or pick up the phone and call me at 415-461-8763. Go to my website (www.nomorecoldcalling.com/partners.html) and connect with one of my partners in your area. We'd love to help. All of us are invested in your success.

CHAPTER 14

One More Thing

What If You're Still Not Getting Traction?

OK, you thought we were finished, but there's still one more thing. Your success hinges on the very first step in the Referral-Selling System—asking for referrals. This is the prospecting stage—the time you spend on business development—and it is the most important step in the sales process.

Unless you are consistently asking for referrals, you won't have the success you've read about in this book. You *must* ask.

Asking is the single most important step in the Referral-Selling System. If you're not asking for referrals, the rest of the process won't matter, because you'll have nothing to follow up. That's why my clients always set goals for the number of people they will ask for referrals each and every week.

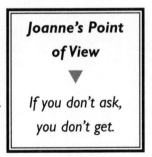

Joanne's Point of View

▼

If you don't ask, you don't get.

We've talked about the importance of creating opportunities and not waiting for them. Unless you have a plan for how

> "Failing to plan is planning to fail."
> —Alan Lakein

you're going to spend your time and unless you are consistently asking for referrals, you will again be in a reactive mode and will respond to every opportunity that comes your way—even if it is a PITA customer.

Planning for Success

In chapter 3 you completed the Business-Development Strategy worksheet based on how you were currently spending your time. Now you will complete the worksheet based on how you plan to spend your business-development time going forward and which activities you can commit to completing. There are four business-development activities: Proactive, Active, Personal, and Other. In the first column write the percent of your business-development time that you would *like* to spend on each activity, and in the second column, consider what percent you are *willing* to do.

ACTION STEP 24

Planning

- Complete the Business-Development Strategy worksheet (see p. 215).
- Review your plan with your Business Buddy.

Business-Development Strategy

▼

Strategy	Activity	Percent you would like to do	Percent you are willing to do
Proactive	❑ Asking for referrals (asking for and getting qualified leads)	_____%	_____%
Active	❑ Mail campaigns ❑ Marketing leads ❑ Advertising ❑ Responding to inquiries ❑ Trade shows ❑ Internet approaches Websites Listings Groups	_____%	_____%
Personal	❑ Speaking engagements ❑ Professional and community groups ❑ Conferences ❑ Networking and leads groups	_____%	_____%
Other	❑ _____ ❑ _____ ❑ _____	_____%	_____%
Total		100%	100%

Key Questions to Ask Yourself:
Are my current activities supporting my goals?
Is the time I've blocked out manageable for me?

Notice whether the two columns are aligned or if there is a gap between the two. If your willingness lags behind what you would like to do, you are probably still skeptical about the positive impact of referral selling on your business. You're going to need to prove it to yourself. So adjust your goals, and once you see how easy asking for referrals can be and the dramatic increase in your business, your activity level will increase substantially.

You now need to go public with your referral commitments. If you have a Business Buddy, you're probably already publicly committed. If not, you need to tell your mate, some friends, and some people in your organization about your referral goals. Then, when you ask for and get your first referral, you can tell everyone about your success. You'll get a lot of high fives and well-deserved praise. And when you make your first referral sale, you'll have someone with whom to share that bottle of champagne.

Keep your plan posted in an important spot in your workplace. Carry it with you. Follow your plan every day. Your success will transform your life.

CHAPTER 15

You Can Do It!

R eferral selling transforms everything it touches—it brings
better customers and long-term relationships, and it
transforms organizations, the sales relationship, and the salesperson. Ultimately, it will transform your business and your
life.

Congratulations for deciding to transition to referral selling. While reading this book, you may have already changed
the way you are selling, or perhaps you're just getting started.
Wherever you are in the process, I encourage you to keep
practicing. Refine the Referral-Selling System to work for you.

A Final Reminder

As you practice, here are a few tips and words of encouragement. Remember the four reasons why referral selling is common sense, but not yet common practice.

1. It's a skill.
2. There haven't been metrics to measure activities and successes.
3. It is not part of most organizations' sales process.
4. People are personally uncomfortable asking for referrals.

The last reason is the largest hurdle for most people to overcome. You may still have some lingering concerns that asking for referrals is pushy, could jeopardize your relationship, or is too "salesy." Here are some ideas for pushing through your resistance and getting to the other side:

- **Practice:** This is the easiest step to overlook—especially for experienced salespeople. Remember my story about exceptional athletes? They not only practice, they practice the *basics*—over and over. Take the time to practice in person with at least three people you know really well, and be open to their feedback.
- **Review your own experience:** Think of all the times when you've willingly given people referrals—even when they didn't ask for one. Recall how pleased you were to be able to refer people to them. Others will do the same for you if only you ask.
- **Ask some friends first:** After you've practiced with three people, ask at least two friends for referrals. The more you ask, the more your comfort level will increase.
- **Keep asking:** The big secret—which isn't really a secret at all—is that you must keep asking. The more you

ask, the more you get. The more you get, the more excited you will be about asking even more people for referrals. It's a self-fulfilling prophecy.

It doesn't matter whether you're a sole proprietor, a small- or medium-sized local company, or a large national or multinational organization—the strategy is the same.

How a Small Company Transformed Itself

Ascot Staffing is the premier staffing company in the East Bay (San Francisco Bay Area) (www.ascotstaffing.com). Ascot has been in business for thirty-four years, has four locations, and fourteen employees. DeDe Cowan is the president and CEO.

Here is Ascot's story as told by DeDe:

> Our sales team was becoming more and more frustrated because our cold-calling selling cycle was lengthening to six months from initial contact to close. Once we obtained a contact name, the process of getting "that magic appointment" seemed to take forever. Sometimes it never happened.
>
> The action of trying to meet the decision maker was becoming even more hampered by the onset of the "receptionist-less reception area." We were increasingly relying on a lobby phone that went directly into the deep abyss of voicemail. Getting in front of the customer to

tell our wonderful corporate service story was becoming impossible.

I was really beginning to worry about the future of our business when I attended Joanne Black's No More Cold Calling workshop. What a breath of fresh air. She put common-sense marketing into a neat, easy-to-use package. I sent my salespeople to her training and immediately installed the program into our company using Joanne's methods of role playing, question asking, and follow-up activities. I realized that any change of this scale had to come from me. My team needed to know my commitment and to feel my enthusiasm.

Specifically, here's the program I installed:

- **Reorganization:** We used to have a staffing department and a sales and marketing department. I eliminated the sales department. My new philosophy is that selling is everyone's job.
- **Goal Setting:** I set weekly and quarterly goals for referrals. Each person is expected to ask at least six people a week for referrals.
- **Accountability:** We have weekly follow-up meetings when everyone discusses the people they called, what happened, and their next steps.
- **Tracking:** We created an online tracking system as well as binders for each person to record and track her referrals.
- **Incentives:** I installed an incentive program for referrals—even the bookkeeper, office manager, and re-

ceptionist have a commission plan. When people make their quarterly numbers, they get treated to a manicure and pedicure. (Our entire staff is female.)

In the six weeks since Ascot Staffing has been using Joanne's system, we have made it a part of every employee's job, and they love it. We always took it for granted that our friends and customers would be touting us. The fact is, they do think of us when they need something, but they don't take the initiative to advocate for us.

Last week a potential new customer called who had simply "heard of us." By the end of the day Barbara, a staffing coordinator (someone previously not responsible for sales), met with the potential client, impressed her, and secured an order. While she was there, she shared Ascot's business-development referral program and asked if they would participate. The surprised HR director immediately said, "Well, my son has just graduated from college and is looking for a job. Would you be interested in talking to him?" That single meeting has now brought us three terrific job candidates and two new clients. WOW—and nary a cold call.

In addition, DeDe says that a Referral-Selling System is the least expensive methodology she has ever seen as a way to create new business. Ascot was paying for the unproductive time during which its salespeople were driving around and working buildings. With so many secure buildings now, it was becoming almost impossible for her people to gain access without an appointment. In addition, Ascot was paying for the astronomical price of gasoline plus parking fees.

Installing a Referral-Selling System is a big change for Ascot. People are in new roles, but when they see the results in their paychecks, they know that they are the ones who made it happen. Everyone has an incentive for the company's sales growth. As of this writing, Ascot is on track for surpassing its growth goal of 20 percent for the next quarter.

By the way, DeDe is the person with the great ten-second introduction (chapter 6), "I'm your fairy *job*mother."

The Referral Journey of a Large Company

You might be a large national or multinational company such as a client of mine, a nationally known brokerage firm. It was shifting from being a high-volume, transaction-based company to becoming a company that built relationships with its clients and added value with high-quality service. Part of its challenge in making the transition was that it had realigned its internal teams to better serve its clients, and both brokers and investment advisors had new responsibilities. Additionally, its clients were high-net-worth individuals—generally people with more than $1 million in assets to invest. These are not clients that respond well to flyers or other forms of impersonal lead generation.

My timing was perfect, as the company had made a strategic decision that the only way it was going to grow its client base was through referrals. If it relied solely on its current clients, it projected that it would run out of new business opportunities within two years, as there were only so many opportunities to expand relationships with existing clients.

In this company's vice president I had found my Ideal Customer. He was an experienced, senior person who knew exactly what it would take to transition to referral selling. He valued my expertise as a referral-selling expert. In addition, I knew that this engagement would be fun. By fun I mean that my client would be open to suggestions and would work with me to craft the best solution. He would be honest and open to discussing successes as well as challenges. He was a cool guy. All of my criteria for my Ideal Customer were met.

We decided to run a pilot program to fine tune the transformation.

• **Created Buy-In:** We met with the key stakeholders in our pilot to overview the referral process and to create excitement for the launch. My client worked internally to inform other influencers about our project. He even spoke with people who might participate in the rollout after the success of the pilot. He covered his bases so that everyone was informed.

• **Announced the Launch:** The pilot was announced and positioned as a positive way to give individuals the tools and skills to support the corporate referral strategy.

• **Created Metrics:** Early on we discussed and agreed on the number of people each person would ask for referrals. Each participant would be expected to bring one or two new clients to the firm every month.

- **Selected Participants:** The participants in the pilot were carefully selected based on their team structure as well as on the strong support of management. Both managers and their direct reports participated in the No More Cold Calling workshop.

- **Built a Reinforcement Plan:** All managers committed to meeting weekly with their people to set referral goals. Managers agreed to reinforce referral-selling skills and to conduct role playing to cement the new skills. In addition, the pilot group worked with me every few weeks on the phone. And each participant chose a Business Buddy for additional practice and feedback.

- **Recognized Success:** My client announced a special offer for the people who had the most referrals and closed business in the following three months. Cash awards were given to recognize referral activities. The client understood that the more often people asked for referrals, the greater the likelihood of their getting qualified contacts.

- **Tracked Progress:** The client installed a tracking system. People reported weekly on their progress, and the results for each team were posted.

As a result, in just sixty days the fourteen people in the pilot program asked eighty people for referrals. They were referred to forty prospects, and have so far closed four major deals. That's a 50 percent "asked to introduced" ratio. That's quite a remarkable feat considering that each client represents more than $1 million in new business.

What About You?

Look at the great successes these companies have had. You, too, can have the same phenomenal success. You've learned throughout this book that referral selling is simple but not easy. If it were easy, everyone would be using a Referral-Selling System. Take the time to plan your strategy carefully, be open to making adjustments along the way, and be accountable for your own results.

You will discover that you will have more revenue, more quality clients who are more likely to refer you, and a lower cost of sales. With the cost of an average face-to-face sales call between $300 and $500 in 2004, it is easy to recognize the value of making fewer sales calls, collapsing the sales process, eliminating the competition, and ending up with your Ideal Customer. Referral selling just gets better over time.

Your sales life will be different than it has been. You can work less and make more money, or you can do the same amount of work and make even more money. But beyond that, referral selling is the best way to have a professional sales life. It's really a virtuous circle—the more you build relationships, the more relationships you have and the more opportunities you've generated to get referrals. I've talked a lot in this book about having fun. I really am having the time of my life. I'm working with terrific people, and I'm only talking to those people who want to talk to me. They recognize that referral selling is the best way to work, and they want my company to help them learn how to transform their organizations.

I've had a long sales career—over thirty-five years. Do I

wish that I had developed my Referral-Selling System sooner? Of course. Do I wish that I'd written this book sooner? Of course. But you're never too old to have new goals. And my

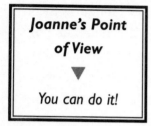

Joanne's Point of View

▼

You can do it!

goal is to transform the way you, every salesperson, and every sales organization works.

You have the opportunity of a lifetime. At the end of the day, selling is about giving your customers enough information and passion to make an informed decision. I've given you the information—the tools, the metrics, the process—and I've shared with you my uncompromised passion for referrals. If I've done a good job, then you are about to begin a remarkable sales journey.

Thank you for choosing to adopt a Referral-Selling Strategy. I've shown you how to get the rocks out of the road. So now it's time for your transformation. Have a great ride!

WORKSHEET INDEX

RESOURCES AND REFERRALS

Advance Consulting, Inc.
831-372-9444
www.advanceconsulting.com

Alliant Resources Group
203-353-0522
www.alliantresourcesgroup.com

Altera Corporation
408-544-7000
www.altera.com

Arbonne Independent Consultant
Joanne Black
415-272-3996
www.joanneblack.myarbonne.com

Ascot Staffing
510-839-9520
www.ascotstaffing.com

Business Network International
  (BNI)
909-608-7575
www.bni.com

California Long Term Care
  Insurance Services, Inc.
650-692-5202
www.californialongtermcare.com

California State Automobile
  Association
415-565-2141
www.csaa.com

Classic Communication
Barbara Patinkin
877-354-1233
www.classiccommunication.com

Communispace Corporation
617-926-4555
www.communispace.com

Paula Doubleday Design
Paula Doubleday
415-455-5301
www.pdoubleday.com

Essex Credit Corporation
866-377-3948
www.essexcredit.com

Huthwaite
800-851-3842
www.huthwaite.com

Integral Talent Systems, Inc.
650-320-8299
www.itsinc.net

International Travel Incentives
949-757-0490
www.intltravelincentives.com

Love Is the Killer App: How to Win Business and Influence Friends
Tim Sanders
Three Rivers Press, ©2002

Mandel Communications
800-262-6335
www.mandelcom.com

M3iworks
408-293-9654
www.m3iworks.com

The Grover Group, LLC
Jeff Grover
440-247-3330
www.grovergroupllc.com

The Marlin Company
800-244-5901
www.themarlincompany.com

The Real Learning Company
800-500-0024
www.reallearning.com

The RoAne Group
Susan RoAne
415-461-3915
www.susanroane.com

Triton Funding Group
Jessica Lanning
415-651-1129
www.jessicalanning.com

For information on other great resources and organizations, go to my website www.NoMoreColdCalling.com and click the "Resources" tab.

Index

CONTACT JOANNE

I would love to talk to you about your business. Call or write:

Joanne S. Black
No More Cold Calling™
80 Corte Precita
Greenbrae, CA 94904
415-461-8763
joanne@nomorecoldcalling.com
www.NoMoreColdCalling.com

Visit my website, www.NoMoreColdCalling.com, to learn more and to find out about:

- Audiotapes and CDs: www.nomorecoldcalling.com/audiotapes.html

- No More Cold Calling Self-Study Workbook and Six CD set: www.nomorecoldcalling.com/workbooks.html

- No More Cold Calling workshops: www.nomorecoldcalling.com/salesworkshop-nmcc.html

- My No More Cold Calling™ providers in your area: www.nomorecoldcalling.com/partners.html

- And, of course, to order copies of this book for your colleagues: www.nomorecoldcalling.com or www.twbookmark.com/business